TRUE STORIES

Journeys of Exploration

Vikas Khatri

PUSTAK MAHAL®

Publishers
Pustak Mahal®

J-3/16 , Daryaganj, New Delhi-110002
☎ 23276539, 23272783, 23272784 • *Fax:* 011-23260518
E-mail: info@pustakmahal.com • *Website:* www.pustakmahal.com

Sales Centre

- 10-B, Netaji Subhash Marg, Daryaganj, New Delhi-110002
  ☎ 23268292, 23268293, 23279900 • *Fax:* 011-23280567
  E-mail: rapidexdelhi@indiatimes.com
- 6686, Khari Baoli, Delhi-110006
  ☎ 23944314, 23911979

Branches

Bengaluru: ☎ 080-22234025 • *Telefax:* 080-22240209
E-mail: pustak@airtelmail.in • pustak@sancharnet.in
Mumbai: ☎ 022-22010941, 022-22053387
E-mail: rapidex@bom5.vsnl.net.in
Patna: ☎ 0612-3294193 • *Telefax:* 0612-2302719
E-mail: rapidexptn@rediffmail.com
Hyderabad: *Telefax:* 040-24737290
E-mail: pustakmahalhyd@yahoo.co.in

ISBN 978-81-223-1327-7

Edition: 2012

Printed at : **Unique Colour Cartoon, Delhi**

Contents

Introduction

Ever since the dawn of civilization, human beings have felt the need to find out more about the world in which we live. Some explorers have been driven by curiosity, some by the need to acquire great riches, and others by the desire to gain fame and reputation.

Though the reasons for their journeys may differ, all explorers share special qualities. These are, above all, the love of adventure and the burning desire to discover the unknown. It is not only the gold they are interested in, but also the way of finding the gold! That is the spirit of adventure that every explorer possesses.

Today, the spirit of adventure, and the urge to expand human knowledge, lives on in space exploration and the quest for scientific knowledge.

This book is about some of the world's great explorers. They set out from their native lands, facing dangers and sometimes risking their own lives, in search of new lands and new knowledge. Their tales will absorb you, and fill you with wonder and delight.

Cheng Ho: Famous Chinese Explorer – an Eunuch Admiral

Decades before Christopher Columbus sailed the ocean blue in search of a water route to Asia, the Chinese were exploring the Indian Ocean and Western Pacific with seven voyages of the "Treasure Fleet" that solidified Chinese control over much of Asia in the 15th century.

The Treasure Fleets were commanded by a powerful eunuch admiral named Cheng Ho. Cheng Ho was born around 1371 in China's southwestern Yunan Province (just north of Laos) with the name Ma Ho. Ma Ho's father was a Muslim hajji (who had made a pilgrimage to Mecca) and the family name of Ma was used by Muslims in representation of the word Mohammed.

When Ma Ho was ten years old (around 1381), he was captured along with other children when the Chinese army invaded Yunan to take control over the region. At the age of 13 he was castrated, as were other young prisoners, and he was placed as a servant in the household of the Chinese Emperor's fourth son (out of twenty-six total sons), Prince Zhu Di.

Ma Ho proved himself to be an exceptional servant to Prince Zhu Di. He became skilled in the arts of war and diplomacy and served as an officer of the prince. Zhu Di renamed Ma Ho as Cheng Ho because the eunuch's horse was killed in battle outside of a place called Zhenglunba. (Cheng Ho is also Zheng He in the newer Pinyin transliteration of Chinese but he's still most commonly called Cheng Ho). Cheng Ho was also known as San Bao which means "three jewels."

Cheng Ho, who was said to have been seven feet tall, was given greater power when Zhu Di became emperor in 1402. One year later, Zhu Di appointed Cheng Ho admiral and ordered him to oversee the construction of a Treasure Fleet to explore the seas surrounding China. Admiral Cheng Ho was the first eunuch appointed to such a high military position in China.

The first Treasure Fleet consisted of 62 ships; four were huge wood boats, some of the largest ever built in history. They were approximately 400 feet (122 meters) long and 160 feet (50 meters) wide. The four were the flagships of the fleet of 62 ships assembled at Nanjing along the Yangtze (Chang) River. Included in the fleet were 339-foot (103-meter) long horse ships that carried nothing but horses, water ships that carried fresh water for the crew, troop transports, supply ships, and war ships for offensive and defensive needs. The ships were filled with thousands of tons of Chinese goods to trade with others during the voyage. In the fall of 1405 the fleet was ready to embark with 27,800 men.

The fleet utilized the compass, invented in China in the 11th century, for navigation. Graduated sticks of incense were burned to measure time. One day was equal to 10 "watches" of 2.4 hours each. Chinese navigators determine latitude through monitoring the North Star (Polaris) in the Northern Hemisphere or the Southern Cross in the Southern Hemisphere. The ships of the Treasure Fleet communicated with one another through the use of flags, lanterns, bells, carrier pigeons, gongs, and banners.

The destination of the first voyage of the Treasure Fleet was Calicut, known as a major trading center on the southwestern coast of India. India was initially "discovered" by Chinese overland explorer Hsuan-Tsang in the seventh century. The fleet stopped in Vietnam, Java, and Malacca, and then headed west across the Indian Ocean to Sri Lanka and Calicut and Cochin (cities on the southwest coast of India). They remained in India to barter and trade from late 1406 to the spring of 1407 when they utilized the monsoon shift to sail toward home. On the return voyage, the Treasure Fleet was forced to battle pirates near Sumatra for several months. Eventually Cheng Ho's men managed to capture the pirate leader and take him to the Chinese capital Nanjing, arriving in 1407.

A second voyage of the Treasure Fleet departed on a return trip to India in 1407 but Cheng Ho did not command this voyage. He remained in China to oversee the repair of a temple at the birthplace of a favourite goddess. The Chinese envoys on board helped to ensure the power of a king of Calicut. The fleet returned in 1409.

The fleet's third voyage (Cheng Ho's second) from 1409 to 1411 consisted of 48 ships and 30,000 men. It followed closely the route of the first voyage but the Treasure Fleet established entrepots (warehouses) and stockades along their route to facilitate trade and storage of goods. On the second voyage the King of Ceylon (Sri Lanka) was aggressive; Cheng Ho defeated the king's forces and captured the king to take him to Nanjing.

In late 1412, Cheng Ho was ordered by Zhu Di to make a fourth expedition. It wasn't until late 1413 or early 1414 that Cheng Ho embarked on his expedition with 63 ships and 28,560 men. The goal of this trip was to reach the Persian Gulf at Hormuz, known to be a city of amazing wealth and goods, including pearls and precious stones much coveted by the Chinese emperor. In the summer of 1415, the Treasure Fleet returned with a bounty of trade goods from the Persian Gulf. Detachments of this expedition sailed south along the eastern coast of Africa almost as far south as Mozambique. During each of Cheng Ho's voyages, he brought back diplomats from other countries or encouraged ambassadors to go to the capital Nanjing on their own.

The fifth voyage was ordered in 1416 to return the ambassadors who had arrived from other countries. The Treasure Fleet departed in 1417 and visited the Persian Gulf and the east coast of Africa, returning envoys along the way. They returned in 1419.

A sixth voyage was launched in the spring of 1421 and visited Southeast Asia, India, the Persian Gulf, and

Africa. By this time, Africa was considered China's "El Dorado," a source of riches. Cheng Ho returned in late 1421 but the remainder of the fleet didn't arrive in China until 1422.

Emperor Zhu Di died in 1424 and his son Zhu Gaozhi became emperor. He canceled the voyages of the Treasure Fleets and ordered ship builders and sailors to stop their work and return home. Cheng Ho was appointed military commander of Nanjing.

The leadership of Zhu Gaozhi did not last long – he died in 1426 at the age of 26. His son and Zhu Di's grandson Zhu Zhanji took Zhu Gaozhi's place. Zhu Zhanji was much more like his grandfather than his father was and in 1430 he resumed the Treasure Fleet voyages by ordering Cheng Ho to resume his duties as admiral and make a seventh voyage in an attempt to restore peaceful relations with the kingdoms of Malacca and Siam. It took a year to gear up for the voyage which departed as a large expedition with 100 ships and 27,500 men.

On the return trip in 1433 Cheng Ho is believed to have died; others state that he died in 1435 after the return to China. Nonetheless, the era of exploration for China was soon over as the following emperors prohibited trade and even the construction of ocean-going vessels.

It's likely that a detachment of one of Cheng Ho's fleets sailed to northern Australia during one of the seven voyages based upon the Chinese artifacts found as well as the oral history of the Aborigine.

After the seven voyages of Cheng Ho and the Treasure Fleets, Europeans began to make headway toward China. In 1488 Bartolomeu Dias rounded Africa's Cape of Good Hope, in 1498 Vasco da Gama reached China's favourite trading city of Calicut, and in 1521 Ferdinand Magellan finally reached Asia by sailing west. China's superiority in the Indian Ocean was unrivaled until the 16th century when the Portuguese arrived and established their colonies along the rim of the Indian Ocean.

The Incredible Automobile Race of 1907

In an article published in the French newspaper *Le Martin* in January of 1907, the editors raised a challenge to the world.

"...We ask this question of car manufactures in France and abroad: Is there anyone who will undertake to travel this summer from Paris to Peking by automobile? Whoever he is, this tough and daring man, whose gallant car will have a dozen nations watching its progress, he will certainly deserve to have his name spoken as a byword in the four quarters of the earth..."

Not only did one man take on this impossible challenge, eleven men did. It became not only a difficult course to drive, but a race. Probably the most incredible automobile race of all time.

In 1907 the automobile had only been around for a little more than twenty years. The vehicles were underpowered and unreliable compared to modern standards. Many people thought these temperamental machines would never replace the horse. Still, there was an enthusiasm about this new invention that is difficult for us to grasp today. If they could be driven the 10,000 miles from the capital of France to the capital of China, perhaps they were more than mere toys for the rich.

The contestants consisted of eleven men driving five cars: Charles Godard and Jean du Taillis (a correspondent for the Le Matin) would drive a 15-horsepower (HP) Dutch Spyker. A pair of French auto dealers sponsored matching 10HP De Dion Boutons. Another Frenchman named Auguste Pons would try his luck with a tiny three-wheeled 6HP Contal. The final, and most powerful car, was a 40HP Itala driven by Prince Scipio Borghese.

Borghese was an Italian aristocrat, but his family had lost much of its money and he had opted for a career in the army. By age 36 Borghese had learned to be a consummate planner and had travelled extensively before the Le Matin challenge appeared. Driving with him would be two more Italians: Ettore Guizzardi, Borghese's mechanic, and Luigu Barzini, a journalist.

It was decided that to avoid the monsoon rains, the race would be reversed and start in Peking in May with the cars driving westward to Paris. The course would take the contestants over numerous mountain ranges and two major deserts. In many cases there would be no real roads, but forest paths and caravan trails.

Prince Borghese used all his planning skills to give his team the best chance of winning the race. He arranged for extra fuel and spare parts to be cached along the route. Before the race started, he took a three-hundred mile ride on horseback to the mountain passes north of Peking carrying a bamboo pole cut to thc width of his car to see if the Itala could squeeze through the tight trails. Where the way was too narrow, Borghese found an alternate route or hired troops of coolies to widen the path.

Godard, driving the Spyker, was perhaps the exact opposite of the Prince. A bit of a con-man, Godard did a minimal amount of planning and sold most of his spare parts to purchase his first-class passage to Peking. He would be dead-broke when he arrived. His partner on the trip protested his lack of foresight, but Godard replied. "Either I shall never see Paris again or I shall come back to it in my Spyker, hot from Peking!"

The start of the race was set for June 10th. The only problem was that the Chinese government, after first authorizing the race, refused to provide the racers with papers to travel through Mongolia. As the race day approached, both Godard and Borghese decided to start on time, papers or not, and risk the ire of the government. After they declared their intentions, the rest of the group decided to join them.

A French military band led the cars out of the city on the appointed day as the crowds around them cheered and celebrated with firecrackers. It wasn't long before the group began to have problems, though. A hard rain soaked the crews in the open cars and turned the road muddy.

Soon they approached the Western mountains that separated northern China from the Mongolian plains. The paths were narrow. In some places the trail was cut out of a cliff with a shear drop into a gorge only inches from the car's tires. Much of the road was too steep for the car's little engines, and mules or men pulling ropes hitched to the cars were needed to drag them through the mountain passes. Once the Itala got away on a downhill slope with Guizzardi at the wheel. The brakes could not hold the vehicle on the steep grade. The mechanic spun the wheel wildly, trying to keep the car from driving off the narrow road into the gorge beside the trail. By some miracle he brought the Itala to a stop at the bottom safely.

After the mountains the next obstacle for the racers was the forbidding Gobi Desert. Pons quickly ran out of gas and he and his co-driver found themselves stranded. They began walking back to civilization, but they had almost no water. Fortunately nomadic Mongolians found the pair before the heat killed them. Pons, having narrowly escaped with his life, decided to give up the race, leaving only the four remaining teams to trek across the hot, sandy wastes. His little three-wheeled car was left to rust in the desert.

The racers kept on track through the desert by following the telegraph line. The engines on their cars were not built with such intense heat in mind and quickly started boiling over. This meant the teams were forced to feed the radiators their own reserves of drinking water to keep them running. A dangerous practice.

Barzini used the telegraph to report back to his newspaper as often as he could. At the tiny village of Hong-Pong, Barzini strode into the telegraph office to send that day's report. He noticed that his telegram was marked as "No. 1" At first Barzini thought that meant it was the first telegraph sent that day. He was amazed to find out it meant that his was the first telegraph to originate from Hong-Pong in the six years the station had been there.

Travel in the desert, as it turned out, was faster than the mountains. It had taken five days to get over the mountains, much slower than a camel caravan. The Itala only took four days to cross the desert, however, something that a caravan did in seventeen days. As the race left the Mongolian plain to enter the mountains at the Russian border, Prince Borghese's team (in the Itala) was in the lead at least a half-day in front of the competition.

Borghese hoped that he would make good time travelling through Siberia. The maps showed a military road stretching across the wilderness. What the maps did not show was that the road had been abandoned when the Trans-Siberian Railway had been completed four years before. The forest had reclaimed much of the road and many bridges had been washed away. Others were in bad shape. Borghese took to running at them at full throttle trying to get across before they collapsed completely.

The race nearly ended for the Itala when it tried to cross one bridge. Guizzardi was at the wheel and Borghese ordered him to drive slowing across the rickety structure. They'd gotten more than halfway when suddenly the planks under the Itala's rear wheels gave way. The back of the car plunged through the bridge as the vehicle did a backwards somersault. Barzini, the reporter, fell the farthest. He found himself under the bridge with a rain of broken planks and debris falling on him. Borghese found himself hanging under the car covered with oil. Guizzardi, who was thrown from his seat in the fall, managed to extract the Prince and the reporter from the wreckage. It was a miracle that all three survived without major injury.

The Itala was in good shape, also. A heavy beam had slowed the fall of the front of the car and spare tires had cushioned the impact of the rear. It took three hours to pull the car from the wreckage of the bridge and get it back on to the road, but when Guizzardi cranked the handle, the machine started right up. "She seems quite safe," he said with a smile.

Occasionally the racers would use the railway tracks for a road. Two planks would be used to allow the car to mount the track with one set of wheels riding on the outside of the rails and one on the inside. At first the tracks seemed a great relief after fighting their way through waist-deep mud and ruts. After a while, though, the jarring and jerking of the auto along the sleepers became quite nerve-racking. The motorists called the movement a "horrible dance."

Once the Itala got stuck on the tracks before an oncoming train. The crew worked furiously trying to get it loose with levers. They got it safely off just in time.

They had been having trouble with the Itala's wheels all through Siberia. In order to cope with the mud, Prince Borghese had wrapped chains round the wheels to give them traction. This worked well but put stress on the wooden spokes making them crack. Temporary repairs were made but the problem continued to worsen. Finally the left-front wheel splintered into pieces leaving the Itala stuck, unable to move another foot.

Fortunately the nearest village contained a cartwright of considerable skill. He managed to chop a new wheel for Borghese out of aged pinewood using only a hatchet. "The hatchet becomes in the hands of the Russian peasant a wonderfully exact tool," observed Barzini. In only a few hours after this major problem occurred it had been solved and the Itala was on its way again.

On July 20th the Itala passed a marble signpost designating the line between Asia and Europe. The Itala rolled in to Moscow a week later ahead of the competition by almost seventeen days.

From that point on the trip became comparatively uneventful. Only one incident caused any problem for the Prince. A policeman in Belgium stopped the Itala for going over the speed limit. When the policeman asked for identification, the Prince announced, "I am Prince Borghese – we have just driven from Peking, China." There was a delay as the policeman confirmed this incredible tale.

On August 10th, 1907, the Itala entered Paris winning the race. It had taken sixty-one days to drive from Peking to Paris. Crowds cheered and lined the streets into the city. "It all seems absurd and impossible; I cannot convince myself that we have come to the end, that we have really arrived," wrote Barzini.

The pair of De Dion-Burtons and the Spyker arrived in Paris 20 days later. Godard, who had been removed as the driver in Berlin over a money dispute with Le Martin, never completed the trip and a driver from Spyker had to steer the car into Paris.

Prince Borghese and the other drivers had proved that the car was here to stay. Others have attempted to trace Prince Borghese's trail, but with limited success. In 1957 Luigi Barzini Jr. asked clearance from the Russians to retrace his father's route, but they would not give him permission. In 1997 a road rally was held to commemorate the race, but the route did not pass through Siberia.

So 1907 race has never quite been repeated. The racers' feat stands alone as one of the most sensational achievements, unequaled, in automobile history.

Crossing the Atlantic by Air

On July 25th, 1909, Louis Bleriot stunned the world by using an airplane to cross the English Channel. He had piloted his Bleriot XI aircraft across the 21 miles of water from France to England in 37 minutes, landing near Dover castle. Bleriot had made the dangerous trip to win a £1,000 prize offered by the Daily Mail.

Four years later, Lord Northcliffe, who owned the Daily Mail, made another challenge: £10,000 to the first men to fly the Atlantic from North America to Ireland or England in less than 72 hours. This was distance of over one-hundred times greater than that of the Channel flight and incalculably more dangerous.

The challenge lay unaccepted until 1919 and the close of WW I. Aviation technology had advanced rapidly during the war, but it was still only a mere sixteen years after the Wright Brothers had made their famous flight at Kitty Hawk.

The first successful attempt to cross the Atlantic by plane was made in May of 1919. The United States Navy had seen a need during the war for an aircraft with enough range and bomb/depth charge capacity to guard ships in the Atlantic against attack from German submarines. Four of these planes were built by Curtiss aircraft and given the designation NC (for Navy/Curtiss). The "Nancies," as they were nicknamed, were designed as flying boats and could land and take off on the water.

When the war ended, the Nancies lost their original mission, but the U.S. Navy decided to use the planes in an attempt to make the first transatlantic crossing. The planes would fly from Trepassey Bay, Newfoundland, Canada, to the Azores Island in the Atlantic, then onto Portugal and England. Such a nonstop flight would not qualify the planes for Lord Northcliffe's prize, but would still be an aviation first as it would require flying over 1,300 miles of ocean, something that had never been done before.

Although four Nancies had been built, only three would attempt the crossing. NC-2, which had been flying poorly, was cannibalized for spare parts to repair NC-1 and NC-4. The Nancies were also altered by adding a fourth engine behind the plane's center engine that would "push" the aircraft while the other engines "pulled." It was decided a crew of six would be used on each plane: a commander, two pilots, a pilot-engineer, a radio operator, and an engineer.

The three planes started for Halifax, Nova Scotia, where they would refuel before going onto Newfoundland, the jumping off point for the first leg of the Atlantic crossing. During the flight NC-4, which was getting a reputation for being a "jinx" plane, was forced to land at sea when two of its engines failed. The two remaining planes went on to Halifax while NC-4 spent the whole night taxiing on its remaining engines to the Naval Air Station at Chatham, Massachusetts. After repairs were made the next day NC-4 flew on. During most of the trip to Halifax, NC-4's engines ran roughly and more repairs were required when the aircraft landed. The next day the plane tried to fly onto Newfoundland, but was forced to land and clear a plugged fuel line before continuing.

Meanwhile the commander of the crossing attempt, John Towers, had decided to start the flight without the troublesome NC-4. As NC-4 prepared to land at Trespassey Bay, NC-1 and NC-3 were trying to take off. NC-4 would have been left behind, except that NC-1 and 3 had been accidentally overloaded with fuel and couldn't get into the air. The flight was rescheduled to leave the next day which was May 16th, 1919. The Commander of NC-4, Albert Read, used the extra time to have a new engine and three new propellers installed on his plane in an attempt to resolve the aircraft's mechanical problems.

All three planes left Trepassey Bay that afternoon, but only after NC-3 left one of its engineers ashore to lighten the load. It had been planned that the planes would fly in formation for the trip, but this proved difficult. NC-3's lights had been shorted out by sea water on takeoff and was running dark. In addition clouds were obscuring the moonlight and NC-4 had a tendency to outrun the other planes. These factors led to a near midair collision as the unlighted NC-3 found itself sandwiched between NC-4 below and NC-1 above. Fortunately NC-4 spotted the darkened plane by moonlight and veered away giving NC-3 room to maneuver away from NC-1.

US Navy ships had been stationed along the route at intervals of 50 miles. They were to fire signals shell and point searchlights up into the air to help guide the planes on their way. Rain and fog soon obscured the ships and lights below. The weather also made getting a navigation fix from the stars above difficult too. At one point NC-4, while trying to get a glimpse of the sea below, fell into a spin and nearly crashed into the water. Finally the fog lifted and Commander Read could see the coast of Flores, one of the western islands in the Azores chain. Because of bad weather he decided to land his plane there at the harbour of Horta, some two hundred miles short of the original destination.

NC-1 and NC-3 didn't fair as well. Both attempted to land on the sea and await clear weather, but were damaged and could not take off again. The crew was rescued from NC-1 by a Greek ship, but plane had to be sunk in order for it to avoid becoming a danger to shipping. NC-3 managed to work its way into the harbour at Ponta Delgada by the morning of May 19th, but the plane, missing most of its left wing, would never fly again.

Ironically the "jinx" plane, NC-4, was the only one of the Nancies to complete the planned flight. It met NC-3 when it flew into Ponta Delgada on May 20th. On May 27th it flew on to Portugal and on May 31st continued on to Plymouth, England. In nineteen days it had travelled 3,322 miles and was the first plane to cross the Atlantic.

While the Nancies were making their historic flight across the sea, pilots and planes were assembling in Newfoundland to compete for the Daily Mail's prize for a nonstop flight. The difficulty of the Nancies trip underscored the danger they faced. Of the three planes that had made the attempt, only one succeeded. The other two wound up in the sea. The longest nonstop distance travelled by NC-4 was 1,200 miles. The contenders for the Daily Mail prize would have to fly over 1,800 miles without landing.

Alcock, Brown and Vickers: Crossing the Ocean Nonstop

There had been nine contenders for the Daily Mail's prize, but only four of those actually made it to Newfoundland. Sopwith's Atlantic and Martinsyde's Raymor were perhaps the favourites to make the first crossing followed by a plane from the aircraft manufacturer Handley Page. The dark horse in the race was a modified WW I bomber called a "Vimy" which was built and sponsored by the British firm Vickers.

As late as March, 1919, Vickers hadn't even entered in the competition. It was only after a young, former war pilot named John Alcock had came to the company and persuaded them to enter the race (and let him pilot the craft) that work on the modified Vimy began. Two 360-horsepower Rolls Royce engines were mounted on the plane to drive it along at speeds of 90 miles per hour and give it a range of 2,440 miles. Two seats were installed in the cockpit in tandem (next to each other) for the two-man crew: a pilot and a navigator.

Alcock would be the pilot, but who would navigate? Alcock was ready to risk a solo flight, but fortunately another war veteran, Arthur Brown, arrived at Vickers in March looking for a job. During the interview Brown mentioned his skill in navigation and how he had planned a transatlantic fight route while he was a POW in Germany. He was promptly introduced to Alcock and offered the job as navigator. He accepted and the two men quickly became good friends.

It was easy to compare and contrast the men. Alcock, outgoing, was usually dressed in rumpled overalls and a gaudy jacket, while Brown was a shy, neat dresser, usually wearing a tie and gloves. Both had served in the

RFC during the war and had their aircraft downed. Both had been prisoners of war. Both dreamed of being the first to fly the Atlantic.

The Vimy was built, tested, dismantled and shipped to Newfoundland in short order. Meanwhile, other competitors were already in Canada getting ready for their attempts by clearing airfields and testing their aircraft. Only bad weather and soggy conditions prevented the Atlantic and the Raymor from taking off before the Vickers team even arrived on May 13th, 1919.

The first problem they had to solve was the lack of a suitable airfield. Alcock and Brown spent days travelling the muddy roads in the area in a borrowed Buick looking for a flat, long patch of land they could use to launch their aircraft.

On May 18th, the Atlantic rolled down its makeshift runway and staggered into the air to attempt the ocean crossing. The plane travelled 1,400 miles before one of the engines overheated and forced the crew to ditch at sea. Fortunately, winds had blown them 150 miles off course and into the shipping lanes where they were picked up by the Danish ship Mary.

One hour after the Atlantic took to the skies, the Raymor lumbered down its field. Overloaded, the plane climbed into the air, but was suddenly caught by a crosswind and dove into the ground. The pilot and navigator were injured, but both survived. With the only other entry, the Handley Page, experiencing mechanical problems, it seemed like the darkhorse, the Vickers team, was now in the lead.

As unfortunate as the crash of the Raymor had been, it was a break for Alcock and Brown. The Raymor crew, now out of the race, lent their field to Vickers for preparing and testing the Vimy. The field was not long enough, however, for the Vimy to take off fully loaded so the search for a suitable field continued. A location was found in June, just outside the city of St. John's. Before the field was usable, the location would have to be cleared of boulders, a stone wall and a few trees. Soon the field was ready and the plane in position, but bad weather in the form of a near gale force wind and problems with contaminated fuel delayed the start. Vickers officials, enjoying a mild spring back in England, impatiently telegraphed, "Please cable reason for non-start!"

The Vimy might have started its historic trip on June 13th had it not have been for a broken shock absorber and heavy winds. The weather improved the next day and tail winds were predicted all the way to Ireland. The wind on the airfield was blowing from the west, however, which meant the Vimy would have to take off going uphill, an added complication since the plane would be so heavily loaded with fuel.

Spectators crowded the field as sandwiches, coffee, chocolate, whiskey and a few bottles of beer were packed into the Vimy. Brown and Alcock climbed into the cockpit where they were seated side-by-side. Between them sat a big battery that would power their electrically-heated flying suits. While a ground crew held the plane back, Alcock revved up the engines. Suddenly the plane was released and slowly it started moving uphill. Alcock had 1,200 feet to get the plane into the air before the field ended in a stone wall. Beyond that was a low hill with trees.

"Depressingly slowly the Vimy taxied toward a dark pine forest at the end of the airfield," Brown recalled later. "The echo of the roaring motors must have struck quite hard against the hills around St. John's. Almost at the last second Alcock gained height. We were only inches above the top of the trees."

The Vimy climbed into the air with only 300 feet of runway left. It cleared the hill, then disappeared behind it and the crowd thought the plane had crashed. They cheered with excitement as the aircraft turned and reappeared roaring overhead, now going east toward Ireland. It was just after 1 P.M. local time.

Alcock and Brown found it hard to communicate once airborn. The engine noise, even at half-throttle, made talking difficult. Alcock found the Vimy a handful to control and was glad he had not attempted the flight alone. Brown kept himself busy checking the engine dials and gauges as well as using his sextant to "shoot" sun and calculate their position. Brown had clear view of it for the first hour, but then the Vimy found itself in a thick fog and Brown had to navigate by dead reckoning. Soon other problems began to arise. A small propeller designed to drive a generator and provide power for the transmitter had broken off. The plane had been silenced.

At 6 P.M. GMT they had travelled an estimated 200 miles and Alcock decided to try and climb above the clouds so that Brown could confirm their position with the sextant. Suddenly there was a noise that sounded like machine gun fire. The exhaust pipe on the left engine split open and melted away. Flames were now shooting out from the cylinders and the sound was deafening. The two flyers were scared stiff. Fortunately none of the fire which streamed back from the engine touched the flammable struts, or wing fabric. The flight would continue.

After 4 hours of flight the Vimy broke through the mist at an altitude of 6,000 feet, long enough for Brown to "shoot" the sun, which was now nearly set. According to the reading they were exactly on course. As darkness fell the cold increased and they discovered that the battery that was supposed to power their heated suits had failed.

"We froze like young puppies," Alcock recalled later, "and in the narrow cockpit we had no room to move about. At any rate," he added, "Brown did manage to get some movement later . . . "

They had been flying eight hours by midnight. The clouds cleared and Brown used the stars to get a fix on their position: 977 miles from Newfoundland. They were past the halfway point. There would be no turning back. The two ate sandwiches, chocolate and drank coffee with a little whiskey mixed into it.

The trip was uneventful for another three hours. Then the Vimy found itself in a storm cloud. Rain and hail hit the plane while lightning flashed all around. The Vimy was thrown about by the wind then forced into a stall. When the plane came out of the stall it plunged downward in a wild spiral toward the sea 4,000 feet below. Alcock tried to pull out, but the controls did not respond. Suddenly they were out of the cloud only one hundred feet above the water. With shock Alcock realized the plane was flying on its side with one wing pointing to the ocean and the other back up at the clouds. Alcock snapped the plane back into its proper flying position, but not before they had come so close to the ocean that the lower wings were covered with salt spray.

Alcock got the plane under control and brought it back on course leaving the storm behind, but it wasn't long before they were back in another one. The new storm was even more dangerous than the last. Snow, sleet and ice covered the plane. Alcock took the plane up to 9,000 feet hoping to find the sun and melt the ice covering the aircraft. Before that could happen the Vimy's engines began to sputter and lose power. Snow and ice were clogging the engine's air intakes and making it impossible to see the critical fuel guage. If something wasn't done fast the engines would soon fail and the plane would go crashing into the sea.

While Alcock continued to fly the plane, Brown climbed out of the open cockpit and onto the wing. He slowly worked his way out toward the port engine which was still spitting fire out of the exposed exhaust ports. While clinging to a wing strut with one hand, Brown chipped at the ice covering fuel gauges with a jackknife. The near one-hundred mile per hour wind tore at him as he stood on the slippery wing surface, nearly toppling him into the black, freezing Atlantic thousands of feet below. With the gauges cleaned, he next worked to clear the intake port. It was a difficult job since he had to avoid the deadly whirling propeller blades just inches in front of the engine and the flames pouring out the ports. When he was finally done, he worked his way back to the fuselage and then over to the starboard wing where he performed the same operation on the other engine. Finally he climbed back into the cockpit for a well-deserved, but short break. He would have to perform the same feat four more times in the next hour before the Vimy cleared the storm.

The two exhausted men finally broke out of the storm at 7:20 AM and saw the sun for the first time in hours. Brown took a fix and estimated they were within an hour of seeing Ireland. Fifteen hours of flight and 1,800 miles of open sea lay behind them. The ordeal seemed almost over. Alcock started a decent from 11,000 feet when ice started to interfere with the starboard engine's radiator and the plane's controls. Alcock continued to descend into the clouds, hoping warmer air near the ocean might melt the ice. It did, but as they dropped though the fog they feared that their altimeter was inaccurate and they might hit the ocean. At 500 feet the clouds suddenly ended and the Vimy leveled out, flying at 200 feet.

They were making a breakfast of the remaining food when they spotted two tiny islands ahead. Behind them stood mountains with their peaks hidden by clouds. They were approaching Ireland. Brown identified the town of Clifden by the masts of a Marconi wireless station. At 8:25 they crossed the coastline. Having completed their transatlantic/nonstop goal they decided to land in Ireland rather than risk going over the mountains in the clouds to get to England.

The Vimy buzzed the town, its noisy engines startling some of the residents. The flyers found what looked like an open field and made a landing, only to find too late that it was a swampy bog. The plane splashed into the mud and came to rest with its nose in the bog and its tail in the air, but the flight was over and had proved successful. A townsman by the name of Taylor was the first to reach the plane and asked, "Anybody hurt?"

"No," was the reply.

"Where are you from?"

"America."

Brown and Alcock jumped out of the plane and were greeted by over a hundred excited townspeople who took them to the wireless station where their success was reported around the world. The Atlantic had finally been conquered and the Daily Mail's £10,000 prize won.

A Life Alone in the Vast Sea

Barbarous Red Indians had surrounded the 'Spray'. They were shouting, "Give whatever you have..." The only man visible on the boat 'Spray' was replying, "No, no..." But they were not listening to him. They rowed their boat nearer to 'Spray'. One of them climbed up to it. He was Black Pedro, a criminal, who was wanted by police for murdering many innocent people. He went inside the cabin. Now the owner of the 'Spray' got frightened. However, he didn't lose his mental balance. He disguised himself and fired at their boats. The Red Indians now got frightened. They could see three men on the boat. Black Pedro ran away. The owner of the boat saved himself.

This intelligent sailor was nobody else but Captain Joshua. He created the illusion that there were three sailors by once changing his clothes, and at other time by making a puppet dressed in sailor's uniform. Thinking that there were three sailors, Black Pedro ran away. Thus, Joshua saved his life and was able to complete his 46,000-mile long sea journey.

Joshua started his journey on 26th April, 1895 from Boston on a 36 feet long boat called 'Spray'. He was the first man to travel across the sea in a small boat for three years all alone.

Captain Joshua was a rare adventurer, who decided to sail across the sea all alone in an old boat. His decision was incidental. Once in 1892, he had gone to his friend's place in Boston. There he saw a boat lying useless since the last seven years. Suddenly 48-year-old Joshua behaved like a youth of 20. He decided to sail across the sea in that boat. However, before embarking on his adventure, he repaired the boat and for many days, he did fishing on this boat so as to acclimatise the boat with the sea.

He started sailing in that boat in 1895. His first stoppage was Gloucester harbour. He stayed there for a fortnight and bought necessary items. Next he went to West Port Harbour in Nova Scotia, where he stayed for a week and secured all his goods for the boisterous Atlantic.

The first week in the Atlantic went by peacefully. To forget his loneliness, Joshua made the moon his friend, talked to the moon loudly and sang songs. His loneliness used to wear off only with the high gaIe. During the gale, he used to get busy in controlling the boat from turning upside-down, but after the gale, the same solitude used to return. By 10th July, 'Spray' reached 1,200 miles east of Cape Sable. He had covered this distance with the speed of one hundred fifty miles per day in the first eight days. By this speed, he soon reached the island of Fayal and took four days' rest. He refused the services of a young pilot because he wanted to experience the happiness of sailing all alone.

On 24th July, he again started on his adventure. But, it was an unlucky day for him. After having a good feast of cheese, butter and plums, he suffered from stomach ache. On top of it, there came a tidal storm. He had become nearly unconscious while fighting on the two fronts when an unknown person helped him. Had that person not helped him, it was sure that 'Spray' would have disappeared into the vast sea. That unknown person helped him to sail till Joshua was again on his feet. And surprisingly, that man disappeared as he had come. To Joshua, this was a mystery and it remained a mystery all his life. He could never come to know who that unknown kind friend was.

On 4th August, 'Spray' reached Spain with the speed of 51 miles per day. At Gibraltar, Joshua was given a warm welcome and this love and respect rejuvenated his spirits.

To avoid any encounter with the sea robbers in Suez Canal and Red Sea, he changed his route to the Cape Horn. But, even this route was not devoid of longshore pirates and thieves. He was followed by pirates. But, nature helped him to outwit them. A strong wave overtook the 'Spray' and shook her every timber. At the same time, pirates were thrown back. Joshua's life was again saved. After this incident, the journey was smooth for three-four weeks. On 5th October, he reached Brazil and stopped at Pernambuco harbour. He met his friend, Dr. Perera and started on his journey on 24th October. Dr. Perera supplied him with the eatables.

With the sea being calm, Joshua's boat was now travelling with the speed of 110 miles per hour. Till 15th December, he had a good sailing. But, at Uruguay, he committed a mistake. In an effort to escape storm, he sailed on to hard sand. The boat lost her shoe and part of her false keel. He had to anchor at Maldonado. The agents of the Royal Mail Steamship Company repaired the boat for free. By 29th December, Joshua reached Buenos Aires and celebrated Christmas at his old friend's place. He had to stay in Buenos Aires for quite some time as the repaired boat was still not ready for the daring sea journey.

On 26th January, 1896, 'Spray' was finally fit to sail. Joshua once again started on his voyage. Twice he was encircled by the barbarous people. The second time Joshua could only save his life by giving all the eatables to them. And the third time again he was rescued by nature. A strong wind blew away the boats of the thieves into pieces and 'Spray' sailed ahead without any mishap.

For three days and three nights, 'Spray' kept on turning with the storm. The storm threw her away from the Cape Horn. Once again Joshua had to face Black Pedro. The latter recognized Joshua and didn't attack Joshua for fear of the gun. So, once again Joshua was saved and he finally entered the Pacific Ocean.

After sailing for so many days, Joshua anchored on 16th July at Apia in the kingdom of Samoa. Joshua organized a feast on his boat and invited the king. On 20th August, 'Spray' stood out of the harbour and continued its journey.

Joshua sailed for 42 days continuously. On 10th October, 'Spray' arrived in Sydney. This was the place where Joshua had many friends. He stayed here for many weeks. He sailed from Sydney only on 6th December. He went to Mauritius in the Indian Ocean and from there he sailed towards his birth place. He coasted along towards Bass Strait and Melbourne at the southernmost tip of Australia. He celebrated Christmas while sailing with the people standing on the shore of Cape Bundooro.

From Bundooro, he sailed to Tasmania. This was done so as to avoid bad weather in Australia. He visited Tasmanian goidmine. The people of George Town gave him a warm welcome. From this snug little place he sailed for Devonport and anchored there on 16th April, 1897.

The season of winter had been peaceful. There was hardly any upheaval. Joshua had nothing better to do except read stories about sea voyage. On 19th September, he reached Mauritius. He look eight days' rest there and he realised that he had almost covered 90 per cent of his journey but America to him still appeared to be further away. In his journey from Mauritius to New Port, his most memorable moment was at St Helena. He stayed in the Royal Palace and spent the night tossing and turning. He waited for the ghost of Napoleon to appear as people had warned him that Napoleon's ghost visited that palace. But his wish was not fulfilled. Next day, he went to the house where Napoleon was imprisoned and hence satisfied his curiosity.

'Spray' sailed towards Granada and from Granada she sailed to Antigua, where the inhabitants welcomed him.

By 4th June, 1898, 'Spray' was heading towards her final destination. And the end of the journey came on 27th June, 1898, after a cruise of more than 46,000 miles around the world, which took him three years, two months and two days. No other ship, during that period, had ever performed the feat for so long. It was, in fact, a 'mid summer night' sail.

Great Fossil Hunter: Roy Chapman Andrews

It was the fourth day of the expedition and Roy Chapman Andrews must have had some doubts. His idea of searching for fossils in the wastes of Mongolia had been controversial. Several scientists had scoffed at the idea of looking for fossils in the wilderness of Outer Mongolia saying that he might as well look for them in the Pacific Ocean. Others thought it was folly to try and determine the geology of a region which was covered by so much shifting sand. Even Andrews had expressed concerns himself on the day he left New York City for the trip. In a meeting with Henry Osborn, president of the American Museum of Natural History, which was sponsoring the exploration, Andrews acknowledged that he was afraid the expedition would fail. "Nonsense, Roy," Osborn had said, "The fossils are there, I know they are. Go and find them."

Andrews was sitting in front of his tent, perhaps pondering these matters, when two cars came careening into the camp. Walter Granger, Andrew's chief paleontologist, jumped out of one of the vehicles as it pulled to a stop. Granger and some other scientists had taken a detour to look at some promising outcrops with the intention of rendezvousing with the rest of the group later at the campsite. As Granger approached Andrews, he reached into his pockets and dug out several items including bone fragments, a rhinoceros tooth and other various fossils. Then Granger announced with a smile, "Well, Roy, we've done it. The stuff is here."

Roy Chapman Andrews was born in Beloit, Wisconsin in 1884. Andrews reported that from his earliest childhood he had a desire for travel and adventure. "I was born to be an explorer," he later wrote in his 1935 book *The Business of Exploring*. "There was never any decision to make. I couldn't do anything else and be happy." He also stated that his only ambition in life was to work at the American Museum of Natural History. Using money he saved from his job as a taxidermist, he arrived in New York City in 1906 after graduating from Beloit College. When Andrews applied for a job at the museum the director told him there were no openings. Andrews persisted saying, "You have to have somebody to scrub floors, don't you?" The director admitted that he did. Andrews took the job explaining that he wasn't interested in scrubbing just any floors "but museum floors were different." A humble beginning for a man destined to become one of the museum's most famous explorers and later the director of the museum himself.

He started scrubbing floors in the taxidermy department and soon was a member of the collecting staff. His first interest was whales. He obtained for the museum a record sized right whale that had come ashore on Long Island. Then he travelled to Alaska, Japan, Korea and China to collect various marine mammals. He wrote two papers about them and at the same time completed his Masters of Arts in mammalogy from Columbia University.

In 1909 and 1910 he sailed as a naturalist on the USS Albatross to the Dutch East Indies. In addition to observing marine mammals, he collected specimens of some of the snakes and lizards he saw. He preserved these specimens by putting them in bottles filled with alcohol. After checking his collection one day, he was amazed to see that the bottles were almost dry. It turned out that the ship's quartermaster, a hard-drinking man, had been sipping from the jars in a desperate attempt to satisfy his alcohol addiction.

While in the jungles of southeast Asia, Andrews had one of his first brushes with the dangers of exploring primitive regions. He was walking down a jungle trail with his servant, Miranda, when suddenly the young man grabbed Andrews by the arm and pulled him backwards.

"A snake, Master! A big snake. There, right in front of you on that tree! You shoot him quick!"

The boy pointed toward a branch overhanging the trail, but Andrews could see nothing. Then a breeze blew the branches around and Andrews caught sight of an ugly, flat head and a black glittering eye. He realized that the "branch" over the trail was actually a python with a girth half that of a man's waist. He could see yards and yards of its body through the thick jungle cover. Backing up thirty feet, he brought up his gun and sent a bullet into the animal's head.

The monster's withering coils snapped the trees they were wrapped around and the animal fell to the ground. The death throes of the snake were so violent they cleared the jungle of brush for yards from around its body. It took a half hour for the monster to die. When Andrews straightened out the coils he paced the length at twenty feet. It had been waiting above the trail to drop onto its next victim: a deer or a wild pig, or, if Miranda had not warned him, Andrews himself.

By 1920 Andrews was ready for a new adventure. For eight years he had been thinking about a grand scheme to "reconstruct the whole past history of the Central Asian plateau" including its geology, fossil life, past climate and vegetation. He wanted to also make a collection of its living animals, fish and birds. In short it would be a complete scientific survey of that vast area called Outer Mongolia. Toward this end he invited the museum president, Henry Fairfield Osborn, to lunch. Afterward Andrews recalled, Osborn leaned back in his chair, lit his pipe and asked, "Well, Roy, what is on your mind?"

Andrews explained his plan and Osborn was very interested. Osborn's pet theory was that Central Asia was a "staging ground" for life. From it, dinosaurs and later mammals and man dispersed across the face of the earth.

An expedition like Andrews proposed might confirm his theory. After he had thought about Andrews plan Osborn replied, “Roy, we’ve got to do it.”

Planning for the expedition was extensive. Mongolia was a large and uninhabited region a thousand miles length and width. In the center was the Gobi desert, where during the summer months temperatures could reach 110 degrees during the day, while at night they would plunge to near freezing. Dozens of scientists with different specialties from cartographers to zoologists would be needed with the group. To transport the researchers Andrews decided to use a fleet of Dodge automobiles. In addition, a caravan of 125 camels loaded with food, gasoline, and replacement parts would be their supply line. This massive exploration wouldn’t be over in just a single season. The scientists would stay in Asia for at least five years, retreating to Peking for the winters.

The danger of Mongolia wasn't just from the extreme climate. Politically the area was unstable. China, which controlled inner Mongolia, was engaged in a series of civil wars. Russia, which controlled Outer Mongolia, was just recovering from its revolution. Neither exerted much control over the region and there was much anarchy. Outer Mongolia was notorious for armed bandits that roamed the land.

Despite these difficulties, in April of 1922 Andrew's Dodge cars rolled through a gate in the Great Wall of China, headed for parts unknown. The first big find of the trip were fossils of a Baluchitherium. The Baluchitherium was a kind of giant rhinoceros that had lived during the ice age. One of the drivers had noticed its jaw lying exposed at the bottom of a V-shaped gully. Andrews discovered much of the rest of the animal's body on the other side of a ridge. The expedition was able to recover nearly a full skeleton, including a huge skull embedded in a block of sandstone. Andrews said after first finding the skull, "I knew it was time to stop for I was too excited to do further prospecting."

The skull and the surrounding sandstone were removed from the ground and covered with burlap soaked in plaster to protect it. Andrews sent it back to China. The party carrying it was threatened by bandits, but managed to get it onto a steamer bound for New York City. The fossil arrived at the museum on December 19th, 1922. Later Osborn wrote that the discovery of the skull and its transportation to the United States was one of the greatest events in the history of paleontology. Until this time the Baluchitherium had only been known through a few bone fragments and part of a jaw. Now scientists could tell what the creature looked like. It stood seventeen feet high at the shoulder and was twenty-four feet long.

The most famous find of Andrew's central Asia expeditions was made on July 13, 1923. George Olson, a paleontology assistant, came back to camp saying that he had found some fossil eggs at the Flaming Cliffs of Shabarakh Usu. At first Andrews was skeptical thinking that they were probably some natural formation, but after tea he and some of the other scientists went with Olson to look at his find. Upon seeing them, there was no doubt. Three eggs and some shell fragments lay weathering out of the sandstone. The scientists were in shock. The eggs clearly lay embedded in rock laid down during the Cretaceous period. Yet there were few birds alive during the Cretaceous and none had been found in the area. The group concluded that these must be dinosaur eggs, the first ever found. Up to this point scientists were not sure if dinosaurs laid eggs or gave birth to live young. The speculation that what they had found were dinosaur eggs was confirmed when the body of a small toothless dinosaur was found on top of the nest. The dinosaur was later named oviraptor. Because of its sharp beak and its proximity to the nest which was full of what they thought were protoceratops eggs, the scientists assumed the animal had been stealing the eggs to eat. It took fifty years for scientists to realize that the oviraptor wasn't stealing the eggs, but guarding them. The ring of eggs was an oviraptor nest, not a protoceratops nest.

The price of these discoveries was the danger and difficulty of working in the Gobi. Andrews recounts that one time the expedition camped on a high promontory that jutted out into the desert "like the prow of an enormous ship." Fossils were abundant along the edges of the promontory and most members of the expedition had discovered something of interest by the end of the first day. They also noticed a large number of poisonous vipers in the area. Some members of the expedition were forced to kill a few.

The expedition stayed at the site for a few days without incident until one night when the temperature suddenly dropped to near freezing. Andrews wasn't sure what snake instinct could have told the vipers that the camp's tents would be warm and inviting, but they arrived "not in twos or threes but in dozens." Norman Lovell, a motor engineer, woke up at two o'clock in the morning to see a huge serpent wriggling in his tent door. He was going to get out of bed to try and get the creature out of his tent, but wisely decided to first have a look around using his flashlight. He found two more vipers coiled around the legs of his cot. Using a pickax to kill the serpents, he got his shoes on to search for the original intruder when a huge viper crawled out from where it had been hiding near the head of his bed.

The whole camp was soon awake and in an uproar. The cook found there was one viper in bed with him. One of the Chinese chauffeurs found a serpent coiled in his cap. Not only were there dozens of the creatures already in the camp, but more were approaching from the edges of the promontory.

Andrews stepped out of his tent onto what he thought was a snake. "I must have jumped three feet straight up and what I yelled made blue sparks in the air" he recounted. Fortunately the object he had stepped on was only a piece of rope. Nobody got any more sleep that night and the next morning the group spent hours removing snakes from gun cases, duffle bags and blankets. Amazingly, none of the men were bitten, although Andrew's dog, Wolf, did get nipped by a small snake, causing him a few hours of sickness.

The expedition stayed at the site for two more days, but despite killing about forty-seven snakes, the number of serpents seeking shelter on cold nights never seemed to diminish. It seemed likely that sooner or later somebody was going to get bitten, so the group packed their equipment and drove off one September morning, leaving this promising location to the snakes.

Possibly the most significant find of these expeditions was not a large fossil, but a very small one. In 1923 Walter Granger discovered a tiny skull embedded in a chunk of sandstone from the Cretaceous period. He labeled it "an unidentified reptile" and sent it back to the museum for further analysis. In 1925 a letter came back from the museum. The skull had been from a mammal, not a reptile. Mammal remains from the age of the dinosaurs were practically nonexistent, and those that had been found up to this point belonged to a group that subsequently became extinct. Granger's skull, however, had come from a line of mammals related to those alive today. The letter begged Granger to "do your utmost to get some other skulls." Within an hour of getting the letter, Granger had found another skull. For seven days all other activity stopped while members of the expedition searched for additional mammal remains. They found six more skulls from several different mammal species, causing Andrews to term the week, "possibly the most valuable seven days of work in the whole history of paleontology up to date."

Shortly after finding the skulls the expedition nearly lost them. Andrews awoke one night with what he said was "a strange feeling of unrest vibrating every nerve." He put on his holster over his pajamas and circled the camp, but found nothing wrong. He still couldn't sleep and soon noticed that the sound of the wind was becoming a continuous roar "getting louder every second." Suddenly the tent was knocked over by the first blast of a desert storm. Fortunately it was soon over.

At dawn the group rose to see a tawny-coloured cloud coming toward them and soon a second storm struck. This one was more violent and long lasting than the first. The tents were swept away and only by quick action did Granger save the box that contained the priceless Cretaceous mammal skulls. Andrew's pajama top was torn off his back and his skin was lashed with sand until it bled. When the storm suddenly ceased, the remains of the camp were deposited over a half-mile-wide section of desert. Andrews stated that fortunately the automobiles had been parked facing the wind, otherwise the cars would have been overturned.

An even more severe sandstorm hit the expedition one day as they were at their excavation sites. Andrews found the dust so thick that he could barely breathe. Not being able to see, he found a hollow were he sheltered against the storm. Granger found safety in a pit, or so he thought, until the wind blew in enough sand and gravel to bury him up to his neck, nearly suffocating him. The sand so severely blasted the windshields of the cars that they had to be knocked out so the drivers could see before the vehicles could be driven again.

In the beginning bandits and civil wars had been more of a nuisance than a real threat. Andrews had equipped the expedition with rifles and carried his own revolver at all times. He even had a machine gun mounted on one of the cars. Once the bandits realized he had guns and would use them, they tended to leave the expedition alone. In one famous incident Andrews was in his auto, scouting ahead of the rest of the expedition, when he ran into three bandits on horseback. When Andrews saw them about to draw their rifles, he floored the accelerator on his car and drove at them at full speed, while at the same time firing his revolver. The Mongol horses, not accustomed to cars, started bucking madly. Andrews later wrote, "The only thing the brigands wanted to do was get away, and they fled in panic. When I last saw them they were breaking all speed records on the other side of the valley."

According to legend, expedition archeologist Nels C. Nelson had a run-in with bandits and didn't even need a gun to escape. Nels, who had a glass eye, removed it and showed it to the bandits who fled in terror.

Civil wars raged in the area, but troops generally respected the expedition (which flew an American flag) and let it pass through the battlelines. This changed in 1926. While travelling outside Peking, they suddenly ran into a contingent of soldiers who could clearly see their flag but to whom it didn't seem to make one bit of difference. "...Bullets began spattering around us like hailstones," Andrews wrote, "They had opened fire with a machine gun but it was aimed too low and the bullets were kicking up the dust just in front of us." Andrews turned the car around and fled. "The bullets now were buzzing like a swarm of bees just above our heads." Houses they had passed earlier that had seemed to be deserted were actually filled with soldiers that were now firing at them. "For three miles we ran the gauntlet of firing from both sides of the road."

Andrews emerged from that incident safely, but as time went by it became increasingly more difficult for the expedition to operate in Mongolia. The Russians accused him of spying. The Chinese became suspicious that the Museum was stealing priceless Chinese treasures. Ironically, Andrews caused some of this misunderstanding himself by auctioning off an extra dinosaur egg as a publicity stunt to raise money for the expedition. It had brought $5,000, confirming to the Chinese and Mongolians that foreigners were profiting at their expense.

Andrews was forced to cancel the 1926 and 1927 expeditions. He tried in 1928, but managed only to get into Inner Mongolia. After the expedition returned, their collection was seized by the "Society for the Preservation of Cultural Objects." Andrews had to spend six weeks negotiating with them to get the fossils back.

The 1929 expedition was canceled and in 1930 Andrews made one more attempt to explore Mongolia.

They found a graveyard of rare shovel-tusked mastodons, along with other outstanding fossils. Despite this success, Andrews finally had to admit that conditions in Mongolia now made it too dangerous to continue the work there. So ended the museum's Central Asiatic Expedition, and with it the golden era of big scientific expeditions. Andrews returned to the States and four years later took over as director of the museum. In 1942 he left the museum and moved to California where he spent the rest of his life writing about his experiences. He died in Carmel in 1960.

Yet, Andrew's legacy lives on as scientists still study and rediscover fossils he found in the Gobi. Sixty years later the Museum would return to the Gobi at the invitation of the Mongolian government and a new round of important discoveries would take place, built on the original work of Roy Chapman Andrews and his brave companions.

Colonel Disappeared Without a Trace

Do you know anything about Bolivia? asked the President of the Royal Geographical Society to Colonel Percy Harrison Fawcett early in 1906. The Colonel replied that he didn't and the President went on to explain the tremendous economic potential of South America and also the complete lack of reliable maps. "Look at this area!" he said, pushing a chart in front of Fawcett, "It's full of blank spaces because so little is known of it."

The President went on to explain that the lack of well-defined borders in South America was leading to tension in that region. Much of the area was 'rubber country' where vast forests of rubber trees could be tapped to provide the world's need for rubber and generate revenue for countries like Bolivia and Brazil. The lack of defined borders could lead to war. An expedition to mark the borders could not be led by either a Bolivian or a Brazilian. Only a neutral third party could be trusted with the job and the Royal Geographical Society had been asked to act as a referee.

Now the President of the Society wanted to know if Fawcett was interested in the position. It would be a dangerous job. Disease was rampant there. Some of the native tribes had a reputation for savagery. Without hesitation, though, the Colonel took the job.

Colonel Percy Harrison Fawcett was born in 1867 in Devon, England. At the age of nineteen he was given a commission in the Royal Artillery. He served in Ceylon for several years where he met and married his wife. Later he performed secret service work in North Africa. Fawcett found himself bored with Army life and learned the art of surveying, hoping to land a more interesting job. Then in 1906 came the offer from the Society: His ticket to adventure.

The Colonel arrived in La Plaz, Bolivia, in June of 1906 ready to start his expedition. After a disagreement with the government over expenses, Fawcett started into the heart of the continent to begin the boundary survey. He quickly found that just getting to the area where he was to be working would be an ordeal in itself. The trail lead up a precipitous path to a pass in the mountains at 17,000 feet. It took him and his companions two hours to go four miles and climb 6,000 feet. The pack mules would struggle up the path 30 feet at a time, then stop, gasping for breath in the thin air. The party was afraid that if they overworked the animals, they would die.

Arriving at the town of Cobija, Fawcett quickly got a taste of how difficult life was in the interior of South America. Disease was common and he was told that the death rate in the town was nearly fifty percent a year. Cut off from the outside world, many depressed inhabitants sought comfort by abusing alcohol. One night one of the local army officers became enraged by his subordinate's refusal to join him in a card game. Drunk, the officer drew his sword and went after the man, injuring him. When another soldier tried to assist the injured man the officer turned on him, chasing him around a hut. The fellow sought refuge in Fawcett's room, but the officer followed him inside.

"Where is that dirty so-and-so?" the officer roared. "Where have you hidden him?"

When Fawcett reprimanded the officer for chasing unarmed men with his sword, the officer cursed at the Colonel and drew his revolver. Fawcett grabbed the man's wrist and struggled with him, finally forcing the gun from his hand.

Bolivia was a lawless frontier is those days, much like the American West had been a half century before. Fawcett, in fact, met an American gunslinger named Harvey. The red-bearded, silent man was quick with his revolver and sure with his aim. Harvey, a bandit, had found the United States too civilized and dodged the Texas Rangers, working his way down through Mexico into South America. He had held up a mining company in a neighbouring country, and there was a large reward on his head. Boliva had no extradition law, however, and he was safe in this new frontier.

Colonel Fawcett was appalled by treatment of the native South American Indians. Although slavery was illegal, rubber plantation owners would often organize trips into the jungle for the purpose of capturing slaves to be used as rubber collectors. Some of the tribes, in return, became quite hostile toward those of European decent. Fawcett believed that if you treated the Indians with kindness and understanding, you would receive kindness in return. During a trip up the Heath River to find its source in 1910, Fawcett had a unique opportunity to test his theory.

He and his group had been warned off travelling up the Heath because the tribes along it had a reputation for unrestrained savagery. "To venture up into the midst of them is sheer madness," exclaimed an army major. Fawcett went anyway.

After a week paddling up the river, the party rounded a bend and ran straight into an Indian encampment perched on a sandbar. The natives were as surprised as the expedition. "Dogs barked, men shouted, women screamed and reached for their children" Fawcett recalled. The natives hid in the trees while the group grounded their canoes on the sandbar. Arrows whizzed by the men or fell around them. Fawcett tried some peace overtures using native words he had learned, but the message didn't seem to be getting through. Then he had an idea. One of the group was seated just beyond arrow range and was told to play his accordion. The man sang "A Bicycle Made for Two", "Suwannee River", "Onward Christian Soldiers" and other tunes. Finally Fawcett noticed the lyrics had changed to "They've-all-stopped-shooting-at-us." Sure enough, the singer was right. Fawcett approached the natives and greeted them. Gifts were exchanged as a sign of friendship.

Not all contacts with the Indians ended so well. During a trip down the Chocolatal River, the pilot of the boat Fawcett was travelling on went off to inspect a nearby road. When he didn't come back Fawcett found him dead with 42 arrows in his body.

People were only one of the dangers of the jungle. The animal kingdom was another. One night while camped near the Yalu River, the Colonel was climbing into his sleeping bag when he felt something "hairy and revolting" scuttle up his arm and over his neck. It was a gigantic apazauca spider. It clung to his hand fiercely while Fawcett tried to shake it off. The spider finally dropped to the ground and walked away without attacking. The animal's bite is poisonous and sometimes fatal.

Vampire bats were also a nuisance in some remote areas. At night these creatures would come to bite and lap up blood from sleepers. Fawcett reported that though they slept under mosquito nets, any portion of bodies touching the net or protruding beyond it would be attacked. In the morning they would find their hammocks saturated with blood.

Near Potrero, wild bulls became a problem for one of Fawcett's expeditions. The group was travelling in an ox cart which gave them some protection. Even so, the group was attacked by three bulls one day. They managed to drive them off only after killing one animal and riddling the other two with bullets. On that same trip Fawcett was fifty yards behind the rest of the group when a big red bull appeared between him and the cart. The Colonel wasn't carrying a rifle and there were no trees or other places to seek refuge. Fawcett was able to get past the animal, as it snorted, lashed its tail and tore up the ground, by moving slowly while fixing it with a hopefully hypnotic stare.

Snakes were also a constant threat too. Once while travelling with a Texan named Ross, they were attacked by a seven-foot long "Bushmaster," a deadly poisonous snake. The men leapt out of the way as the Texan pulled his revolver, putting two slugs through the ugly head of the creature. On close examination Ross realized the snake had bitten him, but the fangs had sunk into his tobacco pouch. His skin showed two dents where the fangs had pressed against him, but never broke through. His skin was wet with venom. The pouch had saved his life.

Fawcett often found it necessary to swim rivers in order to get a rope across for hauling equipment over. The Colonel had to be very careful there were no cuts or open sores on his body that might attract piranha fish. Swarms of these fish have been known to strip the flesh off a man in minutes if he was unlucky enough to fall into the water where they were congregated. One of Fawcett's companions lost two fingers to them while washing his blood stained hands in the river.

Though not poisonous, the giant anaconda is probably the most feared snake in the jungle. Fawcett had a run-in with one not long after he arrived in South America. In his diary he noted: "We were drifting easily along the sluggish current not far below the confluence of the Rio Negro when almost under the bow of the igarit'e

[boat] there appeared a triangular head and several feet of undulating body. It was a giant anaconda. I sprang for my rifle as the creature began to make its way up the bank, and hardly waiting to aim, smashed a .44 soft-nosed bullet into its spine, ten feet below the wicked head."

The boat stopped so that the Colonel could examine the body. Despite being fatally wounded, "shivers ran up and down the body like puffs of wind on a mountain tarn." Though they had no measuring device along with them, Fawcett estimated the creature was sixty-two feet in length and 12-inches in diameter.

Colonel Fawcett probably came closest to death during his trips not from human or animal agents but from the geography of the land itself. While travelling down the uncharted Madidi River by raft, his expedition encountered a series of dangerous rapids. With each the speed of the rafts increased until they were rushing down the river uncontrolled. Finally, the river widened and the velocity slowed.

The crews had just given a sigh of relief when they rounded a steep bluff and the roar of a waterfall filled their ears. One of the rafts was able to make it to shore, but Fawcett's was caught in the current. With the water too deep to use a pole to snag the bottom and turn away, the raft shot over the drop.

Fawcett later recounted, "...the raft seemed to poise there for an instant before it fell from under us. Turning over two or three times as it shot through the air, the balsa crashed down into the black depths."

The group survived, but lost much of their equipment. "Looking back we saw what we had come through. The fall was about twenty feet high, and where river dropped the canyon narrowed to a mere ten feet across; through this bottleneck the huge volume of water gushed with terrific force, thundering down into a welter of brown foam and black-topped rocks. It seemed incredible that we could have survived that maelstrom!"

During a trip to map the Rio Verde River and discover its source, Fawcett came face to face with starvation. The expedition started well: The land around the mouth of the river had plenty of game and the group took what they estimated to be three weeks worth of food with them. Then the expedition was forced to abandon their boats because of rapids, and had to continue up the riverbank on foot.

Because the expedition needed to minimize the weight they would carry, Fawcett decided to bury some of his equipment and 60 gold sovereigns (worth about $300) in metal cases near where they landed. Fawcett was amazed when years later stories came to him about a "Verde Treasure" that had been left behind by his expedition. The story had been retold and embellished so many times that the size of the treasure had been magnified to 60,000 gold sovereigns. The Colonel was particularly amused because the story never mentioned the fact the he had retrieved the cases after the trip was over. He was sure the story would attract future would-be treasure hunters.

As they walked upriver the water, which had been clean, turned bitter and no fish could be found. Then game also seemed to disappear. Soon the supplies they carried were exhausted. For ten more days the group pressed on, despite only having consumed some bad honey and a few bird eggs. Finally, they found the source of the river and charted it.

Freed from the responsibility of charting the river, Fawcett tried to figure out the quickest route to somewhere they could get food. Deciding the best chance was to go over the Ricardo Franco Hills, the group tried to work their way up canyons that would lead them to the top.

The hills were flat-topped and mysterious. They looked like giant tables and their forested tops were completely cut off from the jungle below. When Fawcett later told Conan Doyle about these hills, the writer pictured the isolated tops populated with surviving dinosaurs. Doyle used these hills as the location for his famous novel *The Lost World*.

The expedition quickly found that crossing the hills was futile, and returning the way they had come impossible. Colonel Fawcett instead decided to follow the direction the streams in the region were flowing, hoping that it would get them out. Days passed and no food. One of the expedition's Indian assistants lay down to die, and only the prodding of Fawcett's hunting knife in his ribs got him moving again.

After twenty days without food, the group was at its limit. Fawcett prayed audibly for relief. Then fifteen minutes later a deer appeared 300 yards away. Fawcett unslung his gun. The target was too far away and his hands were shaking, but, in a miracle the Colonel could only attribute to a higher power, the bullet found its mark, killing the deer instantly.

The group consumed every part of the deer: skin, fur and all. The expedition's fortune had turned and within six days they were back in a town with the Verde trip only a bad memory.

For the first three years Fawcett had worked for the Boundary Commission charting the region. When that job came to an end, Fawcett retired from the military and continued exploring on his own, financing the trips with help from newspapers and other businesses. After returning to England to serve in World War I, the Colonel was again drawn back to the South American jungle. As time went on, he became more and more interested in the archaeology of the region. In total he made seven expeditions into wilderness between 1906 and 1924.

Finding reliable companions for his trips had always been a problem, but by 1925 his oldest son, Jack, had reached an age where he could join his father in the field.

Fawcett, by examining records and sifting through old stories, had become convinced that there was a large, ancient city concealed in the wilds of Brazil. Fawcett called this city "Z" and planned an expedition that consisted of himself, his son, Jack, and a friend of Jack's. Fawcett had always preferred small expeditions that could live off the land, thinking that a small group would look less like an invasion to the Indians and therefore be less likely to be attacked. The route was carefully planned.

Fawcett, concerned with others, left word that should they not return, a rescue expedition was not to be mounted. He felt that it would be too dangerous.

On May 29th, 1925, a message was sent from Fawcett to his wife, indicating that they were ready to enter unexplored territory. The three were sending back the assistants that had helped them to this point and were ready to go on by themselves. Fawcett told his wife "You need have no fear of failure..." It was the last anyone ever heard of the expedition. They disappeared into the jungle never to be seen again.

Despite Fawcett's wishes, several rescue expeditions tried to find him, but without success. Occasionally there were intriguing reports that he'd been seen, but none of these were ever confirmed.

So what happened to Colonel Fawcett? What danger that he had eluded in the past had gotten him this time? Hostile Indians? A giant anaconda? Piranhas? Disease? Starvation? Or was it, as one tale told, he'd lost his memory and lived out the rest of his life as a chief among a tribe of cannibals?

In 1996 an expedition was put together by René Delmotte and James Lynch look for traces of Fawcett. It didn't get far. Indians stopped the group, threatened their lives, and detained them for some days. They were finally released, but $30,000 worth of equipment was confiscated. Even seventy years after his disappearance, it seems the jungle is still too dangerous a place for anyone to follow in Colonel Percy Fawcett's footsteps.

Journey of the Atlantic on a Papyrus Boat

It was the early morning of 9th July, 1969. The calm Atlantic sea had witnessed a hurricane last night. Nobody could imagine that this calm sea had grown so wild last night. Only the Papyrus boat still bore the brunt of last night's storm. A part of the boat was still struggling with the waves. All the main ropes and chains were broken. The crew of seven men was paralysed. They thought it to be their end. They had rowed for 46 days, had suffered a lot, took setbacks in their own stride and had managed to come out of it.

Even this time, Thor Heyerdahl, the leader of the crew, did not lose heart. He did not allow the boat to be broken up. He had a mission. He wanted to prove it to the world that how the ancient civilizations had reached ages before Columbus in the jungles of Central America and on the mountains of Peru. To prove this, Heyerdahl had chosen the Papyrus boat because earlier the Egyptians had used the Papyrus boat for sailing on the sea. Heyerdahl came to know of this startling fact from the archives. To confirm that the Egyptians had used the Papyrus boats, he went to Morocco, Peru and Chad in Central Africa. After confirming the facts, the next thing he did was to locate the tribe which excelled in making such boats. He located the tribe, but had to seek permission from the Sultan of Chad to get a boat made by them. The head of the tribe proudly showed Thor Heyerdahl various boats.

Initially, Thor had some difficulty in conversing. The tribals did not understand his language. But, he was lucky. There was a tribal named Abdullah who knew the French and Persian languages. He acted as the interpreter. Before returning, Thor thoroughly checked the power of the boats and was surprised by their strong structure, which appeared so flimsy on the surface. Satisfied from all sides, Thor decided to sail in the Papyrus boat across the Atlantic.

Thor took the permission from the Sultan and went to Ethiopia to get the Papyrus trees, as in Egypt such trees grew no more.

The Papyrus boats were prepared alter studying the pictures on the pyramids. By 28th April, the 26-feet-high boat with all the facilities was finally completed. The, ship was now ready for the expedition.

Six other men joined him in this adventure. They were Norman Baker from the U.S. (the only real sailor),

Dr Yuri Alexandrorich Senkevich, a Russian, Carlo Mauri from Italy (a cameraman), Dr Santiago Genoves from Mexico (editor of Anthropology book), George Sourial, an Egyptian (chemical engineer by profession) and the last but the most important member was Abdullah. The flags of their respective countries flew on the boat.

They started sailing on 25th May. Pasha's wife launched the ship with goat's milk, saying that it symbolised hospitality and good wishes. She smashed the pitcher against the wooden cradle and named the ship 'Ra' in the honour of the Sun God. Amidst cheers, the Papyrus boat started on its great adventure.

For some days, the boat sailed smoothly. No problem cropped up. The first attack came when the wind suddenly started blowing with a great gusto. The rowing oars were reduced to a matchwood. The seven sailors got worried. They took out the spare rudder oar. It was so thick and heavy that all the seven had to help in order to lift it.

For three days, they sailed without any problems. But, from the fourth day, they lost trace of time and the hemisphere. They were not able to get in touch with the

Safi harbour on radio. They came to know about the direction by Africa's big sand dunes. But, the fifth day again proved to be troublesome. The sea was once again in fury. However, this time the sailors saved themselves by being cautious.

Two weeks passed like this. Often they had to bear the fury of the sea, but by then, the sailors had gained immense faith and confidence of each other and fully trusted each other's decision. Moreover, by then, they had realised the immense possibility of the Papyrus boats. It was sailing at 60 miles per day. On 10th June, after they had entered the trans-Atlantic shipping lanes, they found the sea around them filthy. The water was no longer blue. It was grayish green and opaque, covered with clots of oil and plastic bottles floating among the waste. The same day the last chicken was slaughtered. 'Only a duck was left in the poultry coop, but these men did not slaughter that duck. Rather, it was spared and christened as Sindbad.

The night was again troublesome. The sea piled up and became fierce. By the next day, their boat had become more disjointed. They hammered wooden wedges around the mast foot and tightened the mast.

Then arrived 18th June, the dramatic day. The ship had sailed well over a thousand miles around the north-west coast of Africa. The waves were now not merely slipping under them or lifting them up, but were creeping over the stem and pushing them down. The sailors were frightened for the first time. There was a possibility of the boat breaking up into two parts and then there would not have been enough time left for anchoring the boat.

So to save themselves, the only alternative was to repair the boat. They reduced the undamaged raft to narrow strips and fastened it to the surface of the sunken deck. The lifted stem made them control the steering and once again the waves slid under them.

But, hardly had they sat down, it started raining heavily. The whole vessel bent on one side. The starboard rudder oar collapsed, the water seethed in. They had to throw out both the sea anchors and had nothing to steer with. Above all, there was no light from land or ship. Once again their life depended upon the mercy of the sea. This had an advantage too. The sea waves pushed the boat mercilessly towards America.

They relaxed only when they had crossed 40° west longitude. Now, they were in the American half of the Atlantic, heading to the west with the wind at their backs. To celebrate the occasion, the bottle of champagne was opened. For, indeed it was an occasion as now they were very near to their goal.

28th June was a splendid day for the sailors. Each of them was busy in his work. They were either writing diary or washing clothes. Suddenly, Norman wailed. Wild insects (Portuguese men of war) bit him. He wailed and fainted. Everybody rushed to him and was shocked for a moment, thinking that shark had bit him. Dr. Yuri examined him and said that only ammonia could neutralise the caustic acid. But, there was no ammonia in the boat. Dr Yuri then suggested that the human urine can cure it and so urine of all the other six sailors was put on the sting marks, with a rag dipped into it. Norman writhed in pain and convulsions, but finally managed to sleep. Next day, he felt better, but he took some days to recover completely.

The Papyrus boat had reached near South America's shore. Abdullah's words had come true. He had earlier said, "As long as the ropes hold, the boat will float. But if the ropes slacken, the Papyrus will absorb water and we shall fall through."

By the time six weeks had passed, the sailors became so familiar with their environment that they felt as if they were contemporaries of the men who created the Papyrus boats. They were eager to share their joys with the world outside. Fortunately, the radio set, which was discarded when they were not able to get in touch with the Safi harbour, was once again picked up by Norman. And as soon as he opened, he was surprised to see that the world outside was eager to share their experience. The sailors exchanged greetings with the heads of their countries.

Now the sailors were in the last stage of their expedition. But, 9th July was the most dramatic day of their entire journey. The boat broke into two parts from the middle. But, the courageous sailors with a sledge hammer rowed the boat together. And as if sea was also testing their strength, it began to rain heavily. Once again they were riding on a wild beast's back and did their best to save the boat. However, by then the radio contact was made with Shenandoah and Heyerdahl's wife was seen coming on a steamer with a film photographer. The sailors finally took shelter on that steamer and left the badly wounded Papyrus boat into the sea forever.

Thor Heyerdahl was a great adventurer. After some time, he once again prepared the Papyrus boat. This time he improved the boat and made it stronger to bear the wild wrath of the sea. One day this second boat was majestically rolled into the sea. This boat took them near Barbados. But, on 8th July, just two hundred nauticle miles away from Barbados, the sailors had to abdicate this boat. However, they were victorious, thanks to the common effort of sailors and the well-wishers. They were given a red carpet welcome. The Prime Minister of Barbados himself came to receive the brave adventurers, who had created a history in navigation.

To Catch a Dragon

I'd like to catch a dragon," is perhaps how W. Douglas Burden broached the subject of organizing an expedition to Komodo Island with Henry Fairfield Osborn, President of the American Museum of Natural History. Burden, a wealthy, young adventurer and hunter, had already lent his services to the museum on several occasions to shoot exotic and dangerous animals for the museum's collections. He had heard rumours that fourteen years before in 1912, pearl divers that had braved the treacherous waters surrounding a small south seas island had brought back tales of a gigantic, ancient reptile dwelling on the island's steep, rocky slopes.

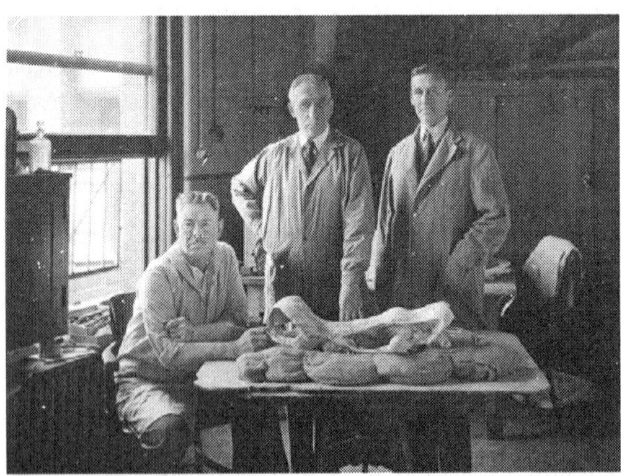

He also knew that P.A. Ouwens, then director of the Zoological Museum in Buitenzorg, Java, had sent collectors to bring back a specimen. Ouwens gave the animal the scientific name Varanus komodensis, but most people knew it as the Komodo Dragon. Burden now proposed that the museum send an expedition to investigate this strange creature and bring back the first specimens to the West. Even more ambitiously he wanted to capture the first live pair anywhere for the New York Zoo.

Osborn was delighted by the idea, especially since Burden was willing to pay the costs, and approved it as an official museum expedition. Burden carefully chose his group for this long and dangerous journey. He found a professional big-game hunter with experience in the jungles of Indc-China in the person of F.J. Defosse. He also hired Dr. E.R. Dunn, of Smith College, as the expedition's herpetologist. Finally, his wife rounded out the group.

Burden not only talked the Dutch Colonial Government (which controlled Komodo at the time) into allowing him to visit and capture up to 15 dragons, but also to provide him with the S.S. Dog, a steamer, to carry him and his group on the 15,000 mile journey. Stopping in Singapore, Burden augmented the expedition with a Chinese cameraman named Lee Fai and fifteen Malay assistants. Then, after a stop at Bali, he sailed for the remote island of Komodo.

As the island itself loomed into view, Burden wrote, the expedition could see it "appeared as a vast mass of torn and splintered mountains." Only twenty-two miles in length, the landscape of the island rose sharply from the coast to mountains several thousand feet high. "With its fantastic sky line," continued Burden, "its sentinel palms, its volcanic chimneys bared to the stars, it was a fitting abode for the great saurians we had come so far to seek."

Before they could land they would have to meet the first danger of this strange land. Because of the island's position in the Lintah Straits, currents, driven by monsoon winds, ripped past the island at up to thirteen knots. These treacherous currents had discouraged other explorers from landing, but Burden was determined to sail on through. The captain of the Dog, to his credit, expertly ran the tidal currents and brought the ship into safe harbour at Python Bay, located on the lee side of the island.

The next morning the expedition landed and started a search for campsites. Because the coastal area was rocky, it was decided the camp should be located higher up and away from the shore. DeFosse and Dunn searched toward the north while Burden climbed westward into the interior. As he explored, Burden soon found hints that the expedition would not be in vain. On the ground he discovered the print mark of a gigantic foot. The shaped reminded him of some of the fossil dinosaur tracks he'd seen back at the museum. Those marks had been made millions of years ago and survived as stone. These tracks were recent, imprinted in just the last few days in soil and mud.

While scouting out a location near a pool, Burden stumbled upon another track. It was an enormous cloven hoof. He realized what it was immediately: The vicious Indian buffalo, a longer-horned cousin of the Cape buffalo of Africa. As he continued around the pool he heard a crashing noise coming from behind him as if "the entire forest of heavy bamboo were being broken into splinters." Suddenly a bull buffalo was charging him at full speed, nose in the air and nostrils flaring. Burden didn't have a weapon capable of stopping the creature with him so he ran. Coming to a steep rock he scrambled up.

Suddenly the jungle was silent. Burden waited. The buffalo waited. Finally the latter gave up and went crashing off through the jungle. Burden had survived the second danger of Komodo.

Within a few days the expedition had established a base camp on a 2,000 foot high plateau. Some existing huts were utilized and Burden wrote, "This hut occupied by the author (Burden) and Mrs. Burden was open to the sea breeze. The roof of woven palm leaves was mellow and bearded with age, and in it contained a rich assortment of crawling life, including pit vipers, scorpions, centipedes, and spiders. Indeed, a most interesting collection could have been made from this shelter."

The expedition soon discovered that this mysterious, tiny island had an astonishing variety of strangely-mixed wildlife. Deer, wild boar and water buffalo on the ground. Yellow-crested cockatoos, pigeons of all colours and fowl of all types in the trees. And also, more ominously, a wider variety of poisonous snakes than almost anywhere else in the world. The third danger of Komodo.

Nearby the camp was a watering hole crisscrossed with dragon tracks, but Burden hadn't actually spotted a dragon yet.

After hunting a deer to feed the camp one morning, Burden climbed into the interior taking the same route he had followed the first day off the ship. Suddenly he heard the sound of falling stones from the rocky hill above. Glancing up, he found himself seemingly looking back in time a million years...

Burden dropped to his knees and crept up the slope moving from rock to rock hoping not to be seen. In front of him stood a dragon. Its great head moved from side to side as its foot-long, yellow, forked tongue darted in and out of it, wide mouth. Pulling out his field glasses, Burden studied the creature from head to tail. Its skin was wrinkled and black with many scars. It reminded Burden of woven steel armour. "...it looked enormous..." wrote Burden later. "He swung his grim head this way and that, obviously hunting, his sharp eyes searching for anything that moved. A primeval monster in a primeval setting."

The expedition started setting out bait for the creatures. This was accomplished by lashing a dead boar to a stake driven deep into the ground. The cameraman could then film the creature as it approached the bait and fed on it. This was a revolting spectacle as the giant lizards would clamp their jaws around a huge section of the carcass and tear off great chunks. Often the dragon would swallow half a boar in one gulp, including the bones and hooves.

Mrs. Burden almost met the fate of the unfortunate bait one morning while exploring with DeFosse. They went out to check on a dragon trap and discovered that half the bait had been taken, but the trap had not sprung. Defosse and Mrs. Burden split up to search for the dragon, but she made the mistake of not taking her gun with her. Suddenly the monster appeared and Mrs. Burden hid in some deep grass. As the animal lumbered forward, she realized that she was standing between what was left of the bait and the advancing dragon. She was torn between running and trying to continue to hide in the grass.

"Nearer he came and nearer, this shaggy creature," wrote Mrs. Burden, "with grim head swinging heavily from side to side. I remembered all the fantastic stories we had heard of these monsters attacking men and horses. Now listening to the short hissing that came like a gust of evil wind, and observing the action of that darting, snake-like tongue, that seemed to sense the very fear that held me, I was affected in a manner not easy to relate."

"The creature was less than five yards away, and the subtle reptilian smell was in my nostrils. Too late now to leap from hiding, I closed my eyes and waited..." Seconds later Defosse returned, saw what was about to happen, and sent a bullet from his rifle into the great creature's neck, saving Mrs. Burden from death at the jaws of the monster.

The party shot several dragons and preserved their bodies for study. The more difficult trick, though, turned out to be bringing some back alive. Traps were built by driving heavy stakes into the ground in a circle, leaving only a large opening on one side. The stakes were then lashed together to form a fence and camouflaged. A nearby tree was stripped of its branches and a rope tied to its top. Fifteen men pulled on the rope to bend the tree over the trap. One part of the rope was fastened to a trigger so that when released the tree would be free to spring back up. The other portion of the rope became a noose that encircled the opening in the stakes. Finally, a nice, ripe, dead boar was placed in the center of the trap as bait.

Normally in a trap like this the bait would be tied to the trigger so that when the animal disturbed the bait, the trap would spring. Burden decided he only wanted to capture the biggest dragons so instead he rigged the trap so he could set it off by pulling a rope from a boma, or blind where he was hiding watching the trap.

Waiting in a small, camouflaged hut in Komodo's jungle was no easy task. The boma was invaded regularly by poisonous foot-long centipedes and stinging scorpions. The men often found themselves thrashing around trying to ward off the creatures.

Fortunately the noise didn't seem to disturb the dragons. After a few hours a small lizard arrived, but didn't go into the trap. Then a medium-sized dragon entered the trap and tried to drag the dead boar off, but it had been securely staked to the ground. Burden decided he could do better and waited. Suddenly the medium-sized dragon stopped pulling on the bait, lowered his head and raced off into the jungle "as if the devil himself was after him" and the party realized that a much bigger lizard was on the way.

The dragon that entered the clearing was an old giant over ten feet long. "Here at last was a real monster..." wrote Burden, "He looked as black as ink. His bony armour was scarred and blistered. His eyes, deep in their sockets, looked out on the world from beneath hanging brows..."

The monster stood still for half an hour watching the boma, practically looking Burden in the eye. Then he made up his mind and charged into the trap grabbing the bait in his jaws. Excitedly Burden released the trigger.

"Immediately the dragon found himself sailing through the air," recollected Burden. "A moment later there was a terrible cracking, for, as the beast fell again, the rope tightened and under his weight the spring pole broke..."

The hunters had not counted on the great weight of the monstrous lizard and the tree to which the noose had been tied snapped off. The animal, now on the ground and held only by the rope looped around his mid-section, was lashing himself into a rage trying to escape. The Malay assistants refused to approach the monster which was vomiting and emitting an unbelievable stench.

DeFosse stepped forward carrying a loop of rope. He'd been practicing using a lasso with just such an occasion in mind. Carefully approaching the dragon to avoid the slashing tail and hooked claws, he tossed the rope an attempt to put a line around the great head. He missed. Calmly recoiling the lasso, DeFosse tried again. It took several tries, but the hunter managed to put a line around the creature's neck. After that line was secured to a tree, another line was thrown over the tail.

With three lines on the creature they were able to get the beast under control. They quickly lashed the animal to a thick pole and carried the 300-pound dragon back to camp. There he was released in a cage composed of heavy timber and steel mesh. The animal, once it was freed inside the cage, worked itself into another round of lashing and clawing. The creature vomited and produced such a stench that Burden had the cage moved a quarter-mile downwind for the night.

Going to bed they were sure that by morning the creature would have exhausted itself, making it easier to photograph and measure him. The next day they awoke to an unpleasant surprise. The mesh at the top of the cage was torn and the creature gone. The great, black scarred dragon had shown that he was not yet beaten by man.

Though the expedition left Komodo with 12 preserved dragon bodies and two live dragons, Burden was never able to capture an enormous old giant like "that one that got away." Still, what the expedition brought back to the museum in New York allowed scientists to study the characteristics of the creature like size, shape and colour, and this added immensely to the scientific understanding of this unusual lizard. The two living dragons found a home in the Bronx Zoo. While two of the skins obtained by Burden were mounted and can still be seen today in the American Museum of Natural History's Hall of Amphibians and Reptiles.

If this tale about an expedition by steamer to a remote, rocky island to find a giant prehistoric creature and return it to New York City sounds familiar, it maybe because it inspired a Hollywood motion picture. After returning to the states Burden told the strange story of his trip to Komodo Island to Merian C. Cooper, the motion-picture producer. Cooper changed the objective from a giant lizard to a giant ape, and added a beautiful heroine, in the person of Fay Wray to produce the classic 1933 film King Kong.

Matthew Henson: Arctic Explorer

The ground was flat and white and cold. In the distance a mist appeared. The vapors quickly resolved themselves into the exhalations of a team of dogs. Behind the team was pulled a sledge. Behind the sledge was a man. The man called his team to a stop and waved down the other sledges that followed. Wiping his eyes he surveyed the desolate, white wasteland. It looked very much like the last 40 or so miles of flat, cold icepack, but something told the man that he was now very close to the objective. And one thing was certain. He was the first man in history to travel this far north. Perhaps a smile briefly crossed his lips as he remembered the first steps he had taken some thirty years ago that led to this amazing, dangerous journey...

Matthew Henson was only twelve when he walked from his home in Washington, D.C. to Baltimore, Maryland to get a job as a cabin boy on the three-masted merchant ship Katie Hines. At first Captain Childs, a square, tall 60-year-old man with flowing white hair, was reluctant to bring such a young lad on-board. When Henson told him that he was an orphan, Captain Childs relented and made the young man his cabin boy.

Henson had been born on August 8, 1866, in Maryland. His parents were freeborn black sharecroppers. When Henson was four, his family moved to Washington D.C.

where more jobs were available. When his parents died, he and his siblings moved in with a nearby uncle. Henson was fascinated by stories about life at sea, so when he saw a chance to become a cabin boy, he took it.

Captain Childs was kind to Henson and under his tutelage Henson became an able-bodied seaman. Childs also instructed him in math, history, geography and the Bible as they travelled to such exotic locations as China, Japan, North Africa and the Black Sea. When Captain Childs died Henson gave up the sea, and eventually found a job as a clerk at a furrier back in Washington, D.C..

It was here fate brought him into contact with Robert Peary. Peary, an officer in the U.S. Navy Corps of Civil Engineers, had already made one exploration trip to Greenland. Peary's next naval assignment, however, would take him in quite a different direction. He was being sent to the jungles of Nicaragua to study the feasibility of digging a shipping canal there that would connect the Atlantic and Pacific oceans.

Peary had brought back some Arctic furs to sell to the furrier and while there met Henson. Henson seemed to share Peary's interest in adventure and Peary decided to offer Henson a job as his personal assistant during the Nicaraguan trip. Henson, eager to resume travelling, accepted and spent two years in Central America with Peary. During this time Peary found Henson's skills as a mechanic, navigator and carpenter extremely valuable.

Peary, who was interested in becoming the first man to reach the North Pole, decided after the Nicaraguan trip to offer Henson a job as a messenger at the League Island Navy Yard in Philadelphia with an eye to having Henson come along on future ventures. Henson accepted. Two years later, in 1891, Peary, who had been granted a leave from the Navy to do more exploration in Greenland, asked Henson join him. This was the chance Henson had been waiting for and he accepted without hesitation, though it caused friction with his fiancee, Eva Flint, and her family.

In April 1891 Henson married Eva and two months later left her to join Peary aboard the ship Kite bound for Greenland. The exploration party consisted of Peary, Henson and four others. One of these was a doctor by the name of Frederick A. Cook. In an unusual move Mrs. Peary also traveled with the group.

The Kite struggled through the icy waters near Greenland to Wolstenholm Sound where the party set up a base camp. Henson's carpentry skills were called into play to build a two-room house that would serve as the expedition's headquarters. The building, which came to be called "Red Cliff House," was completed at about the same time as Henson's twenty-fifth birthday. Peary's wife threw a party to commemorate both events.

In the spring Peary and his men left the camp with the goal of crossing Greenland from west to east in an attempt to find the northern-most point of the island. Peary would then use this information to help him plan his trip to the Pole. Henson was injured, though, and forced to return to Red Cliff House.

At Red Cliff House Henson ran into direct conflict with John Verhoeff, another expedition member. Verhoeff had been left behind because Peary had found him insubordinate and undependable. He also resented the respect Peary accorded the black Henson.

Verhoeff and other expedition members also seemed to have little respect for the native Eskimo population too. Henson, however, quickly learned the Eskimo language, Arctic survival skills and local culture. What Henson learned from the Eskimos and shared with Peary would be key to them later conquering the pole.

This first trip led Henson to spend the next eighteen years with Peary in Arctic exploration. In 1893 they returned and Henson was the only one that remained with Peary when other members abandoned the expedition.

In 1895 Henson, Peary and Hugh J. Lee charted the entire ice cap of Greenland and discovered the island's northern terminus. This trip nearly ended in tragedy as the three came close to starving to death. At first they couldn't locate food they'd cached along the way due to new snow. Then the hunting became poor. They pushed on despite the hunger. Fortunately they managed to find a musk ox or rabbit just as things seemed hopeless. Finally they reached the northernmost corner of Greenland. Peary had planned to do more but was forced to turn back. As they retreated, they had to use the dogs that pulled their sleds as food. At one point Lee lay down to die begging Henson and Peary to go on without him. Peary answered, "we will all get home or none of us will." Lee rallied and they straggled into their base camp two weeks later with only one dog left alive.

In 1896 and 1897 Peary and Henson returned to collect three meteorites they'd found on earlier expeditions. These were sold to the American Museum of Natural History and the cash used to finance future assaults on the Pole. The Peary Arctic Club was also formed to raise more money.

By this time Henson's continuous trips north had worn down his wife's patience. She requested and received a divorce at the end of 1897.

Henson and Peary tried for the Pole several times over the next few years. Each attempt was frustrated and in 1902 the trip was disastrous. Six Eskimo helpers died and the food ran out. They were blocked from progress north across the icepack by melting ice.

In 1906 they returned with a new ship named the Roosevelt after the newly-elected President who was a supporter of the drive to the Pole. The vessel was specifically designed for cutting through ice. The hull was shaped so that if the ship was caught in a frozen sea the pressure would not crush the vessel, but push it upward. With this ship carrying them the first part of the way, the expedition was able to get closer to the Pole than any other human beings – within 174 miles. Melted ice blocked the final distance and they were forced to leave and try again in 1908.

It was during the 1906 trip that Peary spotted what looked like land to him some 120 miles off the coast of North America. The place, which he dubbed "Crocker Land" was discovered to be an Arctic mirage by a later expedition.

While Peary went off to raise support for this next trip, Henson stayed with the ship to oversee repairs and prepare equipment. It was at this time that Henson proposed to, and married, Lucy Jane Ross, who he had been courting for two years.

On July 6th, 1908, the USS Roosevelt departed from New York for what would be the final attempt on the Pole, success or not. Henson was forty and Peary fifty. Both knew they were getting too old for exploring the Arctic. It was then, or never.

Peary had carefully hand-picked his team. It included Henson, of course, Dr. John W. Goodsell, Donald B. MacMillion, Ross G. Marvin, George Borup and Robert Bartlett, who was the ship's captain. The plan was to sail to Cape Sheridan on the northern-most part of Ellesmere Island, Canada, then make the assault on the Pole using a relay strategy.

On September 5, 1908, the Roosevelt reached Cape Sheridan. They spent the long dark winter night there (remember above the Arctic circle the nights are six months long) preparing to strike out toward the Pole in the daylight of spring. The time was spent hunting musk-ox, deer and rabbits for food. Henson made ready the equipment. Donald MacMillon recalled, "with years of experience equal to that of Peary himself, [Henson] was indispensable." Henson used his carpentry skills to build all the sledges and trained the less-experienced members of the group on handling the dogs.

In February, Henson and some of the Eskimos travelled by sledge to Cape Columbia which would serve as a base camp for the attempt. They built several igloos and cached supplies there. Soon the rest of the group joined them.

On March 1, 1909, Henson pointed his sledge north and, under Peary's orders, stated breaking the trail across the icepack toward the pole. Bartlett and Borup had left the day before.

There are few activities more dangerous than Arctic exploration on land. One of those, though, is Arctic exploration on the icepack. While travelling across the icepack there are all the hazards of the far northern climate: Sub-freezing temperatures, sudden storms, slow starvation, plus those particular to the great ice sheets that cover the Arctic Ocean.

One might picture that with the low temperatures near the North Pole the ice there must be thick, hard and smooth. Nothing could be farther from the truth. The movement of currents under the icepack cause constant changes on it's surface. Small, steep mountains of ice, called "pressure ridges" well up blocking the path. Sections of the pack are often rent apart creating open lanes of water called "leads." Anyone slipping into a lead can drown, or freeze to death in minutes.

Henson, and the rest of Peary's party, constantly ran into these dangerous obstacles. Peary fell into leads twice during the trip. Henson also slipped into one and was rescued just in time by his Eskimo assistant Ootah. Bartlett and his team nearly floated out to sea on an ice island formed by leads opening around their igloo in the middle of the night. Fortunately they were able to dash to safety.

Each of the Americans knew that not all of them would be able to go all the way with Peary to the Pole. The plan called for each team to go so far along the path, then cache the supplies it was carrying to be used by the other teams going closer to the Pole. However Peary had stated from the beginning that "Henson must go all the way. I can't make it there without him." Perhaps this was to fulfill a promise that Henson Peary had made when Henson had saved his life in Greenland years ago, but more likely it was because Henson was simply the best and most skillful of Peary's assistants. His loyalty and dependability had been proven over twenty years of exploration. Still, Henson knew he would only go to the Pole if conditions were right. Injury or sickness could easily force a change in plans.

As supplies ran out teams started to turn back. The first were those led by MacMillan and Goodsell. Then Borup. Then Marvin.

Henson went to Marvin's igloo to say goodbye, expecting to see him back on the ship. He never did.

Marvin died on the return trip. His Eskimo companions said that he fell into an open lead and they were unable to rescue him. Later, one of them admitted he had killed Marvin in a dispute. The murder was probably brought on by the tension of the dangerous return trip and the inability of the American and Eskimos to communicate clearly.

The final team to turn back was Bartlett's. Bartlett had wanted to go on to the Pole, but admitted "Henson was a better dog driver than I." It was Henson's observation that "Captain Bartlett was glad to turn back when he did. He frankly told me several times that he had little expectation of ever returning alive."

Bartlett did make it back to the ship, but his fear of death was well-founded. As the Arctic spring continued, the icepack grew softer and more leads opened. The only way to get past a long, wide lead was to wait for it to freeze over again. If a big one opened behind the explorers, they might well starve to death as they waited for the lead to close.

Henson and Peary were only 174 miles from the Pole. They drove forward at an almost reckless pace. Peary used his sextant and chronometer-watch to constantly check their progress. Henson, using his astounding ability to reach a destination through "dead reckoning" broke the trail. He had once won a bet with Peary by estimating their position in his head to within twenty miles after a thousand mile trip. Now he let his sense of direction guide him north.

Five days after they had separated from Bartlett, they arrived at the top of the world. Peary made numerous measurements to check his position. Then they found a thin section of ice and broke through to do a sounding. The rope ran out at 9,000 feet. This surprised them as they hadn't thought the ocean would be so deep at the Pole.

Then they started the return. They were exhausted, but the planning they had put into the expedition paid off. With igloos and supplies already in position, they made the return to the base camp at Cape Columbia in record time. Four hundred and thirteen miles in sixteen days. When they finally arrived, Henson and Peary went to their igloos and collapsed in exhaustion.

It took until July for the Roosevelt to free itself from the ice and start working its way south. On August 17th the ship put in at Etah, Greenland. Here the party heard some startling news. Dr. Frederick A. Cook, the same man who had been with Henson and Peary on an earlier Greenland trip, was claiming that he had reached the Pole on April 21, 1908, a full year before Peary's party.

The group was at first stunned, then skeptical. Henson interviewed the two Eskimos that supposedly had gone with Cook. They laughed, admitting they had never gone more than 20 miles out on the icepack. An examination of Cook's sledge, which was still at Etah, showed it had hardly been used. It seemed obvious the Cook was telling a bold-faced lie.

A simple honour system had governed Arctic exploration, and Cook took full advantage of it. By the time Peary had returned to the U.S., Cook had already received several honours in Europe and his success had been accepted by the public. Upon hearing Peary's charges against Cook, the National Geographic Society investigated and determined that Cook's claim was a hoax. A sea captain came forward and testified that he'd been paid by Cook to produce sextant readings that would be consistent with being taken at the North Pole.

Exposed, Cook disappeared. Eventually, in a separate matter, he was convicted and sent to jail for 14 years for selling bogus oil well stocks.

Decades after both Peary and Henson died, claims were made that they had gotten lost on their way to the Pole and missed it by a hundred miles. These claims, though, had little evidence to back them up. Peary took numerous sightings with his sextant to check his position and was as close to the Pole as his instrument would allow: about five miles. The position can be confirmed by looking at the sounding they did. The North Pole lays over a deep marine trench. Peary's sounding showed the depth was over 9,000 feet. If the Peary party had been carried west by drifting ice, as some believe, they would have been over shallower water. Further evidence can be found through a technique known as photogrammetic rectification. Photogrammetic rectification can be used to examine a picture and determine from the angle of shadows at what latitude the photo was taken. The photos taken by Peary have been analyzed and prove the expedition was truly at the Pole.

Unfortunately Cook's hoax stole much of the enthusiasm that the public might have had for the expedition's success. Eventually Peary was properly honoured, but Henson, as a black man, got little recognition.

It wasn't until 1937, at age seventy, that Henson got some of the attention he deserved. In that year he was made an honourary member of the famed Explorers Club in New York. In 1946 he was honoured by the U.S. Navy with a medal. His most-prized award, though, was a gold medal from the Chicago Geographic Society.

Henson died on March 9th, 1955, and was buried in a small plot at the Woodlawn Cemetery in the Bronx. In 1987, Dr. S. Allen Counter, a Henson biographer, led a movement to have the remains of both Henson and his wife moved to lay adjacent to Robert Peary in Arlington National Cemetery, a more fitting location for an American hero. President Ronald Reagan granted permission and on the seventy-ninth anniversary of the discovery of the North Pole, Henson was laid to rest near his old friend. On Henson's tomb is written a quote from his autobiography:

"The lure of the Arctic is tugging at my heart. To me the trail is calling. The old trail. The trail that is always new".

IBN Battuta - The Great Traveller

Ibn Battuta also known as Shams ad-Din was a Muslim Moroccan explorer, known for his extensive travels published in the Rihla (literally, "The Journey"). Over a period of thirty years, he visited most of the known Islamic world, including North Africa, the Horn of Africa, West Africa, Southern Europe and Eastern Europe in the West, to the Middle East, South Asia, Central Asia, Southeast Asia and China in the East, a distance surpassing his near-contemporary Marco Polo. Ibn Battuta is considered one of the greatest travellers of all time. He journeyed more than 75,000 miles (121,000 km), a figure unsurpassed by any individual explorer until the coming of the Steam Age some 450 years later.

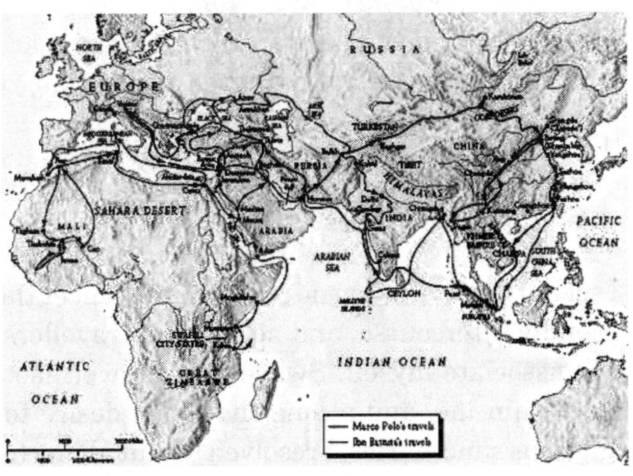

The Rihla (the journey) supplies biographical background. Ibn Battuta was born into a Berber family of Islamic legal scholars in Tangier, Morocco, on 25 February 1304, during the reign of the Marinid dynasty. As a young man he would have studied at a Sunni Maliki madhhab, (Islamic jurisprudence school), the dominant form of education in North Africa at that time. In June 1325, at the age of twenty-one, Ibn Battuta set off from his hometown on a hajj, or pilgrimage, to Mecca, a journey that would take sixteen months. He would not see Morocco again for twenty-four years.

"I set out alone, finding no companion to cheer the way with friendly intercourse, and no party of travellers with whom to associate myself. Swayed by an overmastering impulse within me, and a long-cherished desire to visit those glorious sanctuaries, I resolved to quit all my friends and tear myself away from my home. As my parents were still alive, it weighed grievously upon me to part from them, and both they and I were afflicted with sorrow."

He travelled to Mecca overland, following the North African coast across the sultanates of Abd al-Wadid and Hafsid. The route took him through Tlemcen, Béjaïa and then Tunis where he stayed for two months. For safety, Ibn Battuta usually joined a caravan to reduce the risk of an attack by wandering Arab bedouin. He took a bride in the town of Sfax, the first in a series of marriages that would feature in his travels.

In the early spring of 1326, after a journey of over 3,500 km (2,200 mi), Ibn Battuta arrived at the port of Alexandria, then part of the Bahri Mamluk empire. He spent several weeks visiting sites in the area then headed inland to Cairo, the capital of the Mamluk Sultanate and even at that time an important large city. After spending about a month in Cairo, he embarked on the first of many detours within the relative safety of Mamluk territory. Of the three usual routes to Mecca, Ibn Battuta chose the least-travelled, which involved a journey up the Nile valley, then east to the Red Sea port of Aydhab, Upon approaching the town however, a local rebellion forced him to turn back.

Ibn Battuta returned to Cairo and took a second side trip, this time to Mamluk-controlled Damascus. During his first trip he had encountered a holy man, Shaykh Abul Hasan al Shadili, who prophesied that he would only reach Mecca by travelling through Syria. The diversion held an added advantage; due to the holy places that lay along the way, including Hebron, Jerusalem, and Bethlehem, the Mamluk authorities spared no efforts in keeping the route safe for pilgrims. Without this help many travellers would be robbed and murdered.

After spending the Muslim month of Ramadan in Damascus, he joined a caravan travelling the 1,500 km (930 mi) south to Medina, burial place of the Islamic prophet Muhammad. After four days in the town, he journeyed on to Mecca where completing his pilgrimage he took the honourific status of El-Hajji. Rather than return home, Ibn Battuta instead decided to continue on, choosing as his next destination the Ilkhanate, a Mongol Khanate, to the northeast.

On 17 November 1326, following a month spent in Mecca, Ibn Battuta joined a large caravan of pilgrims returning to Iraq across the Arabian Peninsula. The group headed north to Medina and then, travelling at night, turned northeast across the Nejd plateau to Najaf, on a journey that lasted about two weeks. In Najaf he visited the mausoleum of Ali ibn Abi Talib (Ali), the first Shi'a Imam, a site venerated by the Shi'a community to this day.

Then, instead of continuing on to Baghdad with the caravan, Ibn Battuta started a six-month detour that took him into Persia. From Najaf he journeyed to Wasit then followed the river Tigris south to Basra. His next destination was the town of Esfahan across the Zagros Mountains in Persia. He then headed south to Shiraz, a large flourishing city spared the destruction wrought by Mongol invaders on many more northerly towns. Finally, he returned across the mountains to Baghdad, arriving there in June 1327. Parts of the city were still ruined from the damage inflicted by Hulago Khan's invading army in 1255.

In Baghdad he found Abu Sa'id, the last Mongol ruler of the unified Ilkhanate, leaving the city and heading north with a large retinue. Ibn Battuta joined the royal caravan for a while, then turned north on the Silk Road to Tabriz, the first major city in the region to open its gates to the Mongols and by then an important trading center as most of its nearby rivals had been razed by the Mongol invaders.

Ibn Battuta left again for Baghdad, probably in July, but first took an excursion northwards along the river Tigris, visiting Mosul, Cizre and Mardin, in modern day Iraq and Turkey. Once back in Mosul, he joined a "feeder" caravan of pilgrims heading south to Baghdad where they would meet up with the main caravan that crossed the Arabian Desert to Mecca. Ill with diarrhea, he arrived in the city weak and exhausted for his second hajj.

Ibn Battuta remained in Mecca for some time (the Rihla suggests about three years, from September 1327 until autumn 1330). Problems with chronology however, lead commentators to suggest that he may have left after the 1328 hajj.

After the hajj in either 1328 or 1330, he made his way to the port of Jeddah on the Red Sea coast. From there he followed the coast in a series of boats making slow progress against the prevailing south-easterly winds. Once in the Yemen he visited Zabid and later the highland town of Ta'izz, where he met the Rasulid dynasty king (Malik) Mujahid Nur al-Din Ali. Ibn Battuta also mentions visiting Sana'a, but whether he actually did so is doubtful. In all likelihood, he went directly from Ta'izz to the important trading port of Aden, arriving around the beginning of 1329 or 1331.

From Aden, Ibn Battuta embarked on a ship heading for Zeila on the coast of Somalia. He then moved on to Cape Guardafui further down the Somalia seaboard, spending about a week in each location. Later he would visit Mogadishu, the then pre-eminent city of the "Land of the Berbers" (Bilad al Barbar, the medieval Arabic term for the Horn of Africa).

When he arrived in 1331, Mogadishu stood at the zenith of its prosperity. Ibn Battuta described it as "an exceedingly large city" with many rich merchants, noted for its high quality fabric that was exported to other countries including Egypt. He added that the city was ruled by a Somali Sultan, originally from Berbera in northern Somalia, who spoke both Somali (referred to as Mogadishan, the Benadir dialect of Somali) and Arabic with equal fluency. The Sultan also had a retinue of wazirs (ministers), legal experts, commanders, royal eunuchs, and assorted hangers-on at his beck and call.

Battuta continued by ship south to the Swahili Coast, a region then known in Arabic as the Bilad al-Zanj ("Land of the Zanj"), with an overnight stop at the island town of Mombasa. Although relatively small at the time, Mombasa would become important in the following century. After a journey along the coast, Ibn Battuta next arrived in the island town of Kilwa in present day Tanzania, which had become an important transit center of the gold trade. He described the city as "one of the most beautiful and well-constructed towns in the world".

Ibn Battuta recorded his visit to the Kilwa Sultanate in 1330, and commented favourably on the humility and religion of its ruler, Sultan al-Hasan ibn Sulaiman, a descendant of the legendary Ali ibn al-Hassan Shirazi. He further wrote that the authority of the Sultan extended from Malindi in the north to Inhambane in the south and was particularly impressed by the planning of the city, believing it to be the reason for Kilwa's success along the coast. From this period date the construction of the

Palace of Husuni Kubwa and a significant extension to the Great Mosque of Kilwa, which was made of Coral Stones the largest Mosque of its kind. With a change in the monsoon winds, Ibn Battuta sailed back to Arabia, first to Oman and the Strait of Hormuz then on to Mecca for the hajj of 1330 (or 1332).

After spending another year in Mecca, Ibn Battuta decided to seek employment with the Muslim Sultan of Delhi, Muhammad bin Tughluq. In 1330 (or 1332), in need of a guide and translator for his journey, he set off for the Seljuq controlled territory of Anatolia to join one of the caravans that went from there to India. From the Syrian port of Latakia, a Genoese ship took him to Alanya on the southern coast of modern-day Turkey. He then travelled overland to Konya and afterwards to Sinope on the Black Sea coast.

From Sinope he took a sea route to Crimea, arriving so in the Golden Horde realm. He went to port town of Azov, where he met with emir of the Khan, then to the large and rich city of Majar. He left Majar to meet with Uzbeg Khan travelling court (horde), which was in the time near Beshtau mountain. From there he made a journey to Bolghar, which became the northernmost point he reached, and noted its unusually (for subtropics dweller) short nights in summer. Then he returned to Khan's court and with it moved to Astrakhan.

When they reached Astrakhan, Uzbeg Khan had just given permission for one of his pregnant wives, Princess Bayalun, a daughter of Byzantine Emperor Andronikos III Palaiologos, to return to her home city of Constantinople to give birth. Ibn Battuta talked his way into this expedition, which would be his first beyond the boundaries of the Islamic world.

Arriving in Constantinople towards the end of 1332 (or 1334), he met the Byzantine emperor Andronikos III Palaiologos. He visited the great church of Hagia Sophia and spoke with a Christian Orthodox priest about his travels in the city of Jerusalem. After a month in the city, Ibn Battuta returned to Astrakhan, then arrived in the capital city Sarai al-Jadid and reported his travelling account to Sultatn Mohammad Uzbek. Thereafter he continued past the Caspian and Aral Seas to Bukhara and Samarkand. From there, he journeyed south to Afghanistan, then crossed into India via the mountain passes of the Hindu Kush. In the Rihla he mentions these mountains and the history of the range.

Muhammad Ibn Tughluq was renowned as the wealthiest man in the Muslim World at that time. He patronised various scholars, sufis, Qadis, Viziers and other functionaries in order to consolidate his rule. As with Mamluk Egypt, the Tughlaq Dynasty was a rare vestigial example of Muslim rule in Asia after the Mongol Invasion. On the strength of his years of study in Mecca, Ibn Battuta was appointed a Qadi, or judge, by the Sultan. He found it difficult to enforce Islamic laws beyond the Sultan's court in Delhi due to lack of Islamic appeal in India.

From the Rajput Kingdom of Sarsatti, he visited Hansi in India, describing it as "among the most beautiful cities, the best constructed and the most populated; it is surrounded with a strong wall, and its founder is said to be one of the great infidel kings, called Tara". Upon his arrival in Sindh, Ibn Battuta mentions the Indian Rhinoceros that lived on the banks of the Indus River.

The Sultan was erratic even by the standards of the time, and for six years Ibn Battuta veered between living the high life of a trusted subordinate, and falling under suspicion of treason for a variety of offences. His plan to leave on the pretext of taking another hajj was stymied by the Sultan who asked him to instead become his ambassador to Yuan Dynasty China. Given the opportunity to get away from the Sultan and visit new lands, he readily accepted.

En route to the coast at the start of his journey to China, Ibn Battuta and his party were attacked by a group of Hindus. Separated from his companions, he was robbed and nearly lost his life. Despite this setback, within ten days he had caught up with his group and continued on to Khambhat in the Indian state of Gujarat. From there, they sailed to Kozhikode (Calicut), where Portuguese explorer Vasco da Gama would land two centuries later. While Ibn Battuta visited a mosque on shore, a storm arose, and one of the ships of his expedition was sunk. The other ship then sailed without him only to be seized by a local Sumatran king a few months later .

Afraid to return to Delhi and be seen as a failure, he stayed for a time in southern India under the protection of Jamal-ud-Din, ruler of the small but powerful Nawayath sultanate on the banks of the Sharavathi River next to the Arabian Sea. This area is today known as Hosapattana and lies in the Honavar administrative district of Uttara Kannada. Following the overthrow of the sultanate, Ibn Battuta had no choice but to leave India. Although determined to continue the journey to China, he first took a detour to visit the Maldive Islands.

He spent nine months on the islands, much longer than he had intended. As a Chief Qadi, his skills were highly desirable in the formerly Buddhist nation that had recently converted to Islam. Half-kidnapped into staying, he became chief judge and married into the royal family of Omar I. He became embroiled in local politics and left when his strict judgments in the laissez-faire island kingdom began to chafe with its rulers. In the Rihla he mentions his dismay at the local women going about with no clothing above the waist, and the locals taking no notice when he complained. From the Maldives, he carried on to Sri Lanka and visited Sri Pada and Tenavarai temple.

Ibn Battuta's ship almost sank on embarking from Sri Lanka, only for the vessel that came to his rescue to suffer an attack by pirates. Stranded on shore, he worked his way back to Kozhikode, from where he returned to the Maldives and boarded a Chinese junk, still intending to reach China and take up his ambassadorial post.

He reached the port of Chittagong in modern-day Bangladesh intending to travel to Sylhet. Ibn Battuta went further north into Assam, then turned around and continued with his original plan.

In the year 1346 Ibn Battuta travelled on to Sumatra Indonesia where he notes in his travel log, that the ruler of Samudera Pasai was a Muslim, who performs his religious duties in his utmost zeal. The madh'hab he observed was Imam Shafi'i with the similar customs he had seen in coastal India especially among the Mappila Muslim (who were also the followers of Imam Shafi'i). Ibn Battuta then sailed to Malacca, Vietnam, the Philippines and finally Quanzhou in Fujian Province, China.

On arriving in China in the year 1345, one of the first things he notes is the local artists and their mastery in making portraitures of newly arrived foreigners. Ibn Battuta also mentions Chinese cuisine and its usage of animals such as frogs. While in Quanzhou he ascended the "Mount of the Hermit" and briefly visited a well-known Taoist monk. From there, he went north to Hangzhou, which he describes it as one of the largest cities he has ever seen, and he noted its charm, describes the city sat on a beautiful lake and is surrounded by gentle green hills. During his stay at Hangzhou, he was particularly impressed by the large number of well-crafted and well-painted Chinese wooden ships with coloured sails and silk awnings assembling in the canals later he attends a banquet of the Yuan Mongol administrator of the city named Qurtai, who according to Ibn Battuta, was very fond of the skills of local Chinese conjurers. He also described travelling further north, through the Grand Canal to Beijing, but as he neared the capital an internal power struggle among the Yuan Mongols erupted, causing Ibn Battuta and his Hui guides to return to the south coast. On boarding a Chinese Junk heading for Southeast Asia, Ibn Battuta was unfairly charged a hefty sum by the crew and lost much of what he had collected during his stay in China. Ibn Battuta also reported "the rampart of Yajuj and Majuj" was "sixty days' travel" from the city of Zeitun (Quanzhou); Hamilton Alexander Rosskeen Gibb notes that Ibn Battuta believed that Great Wall of China was built by Dhul-Qarnayn to contain Gog and Magog as mentioned in the Quran.

After returning to Quanzhou in 1346, Ibn Battuta began his journey back to Morocco. In Kozhikode, he once again considered throwing himself at the mercy of Muhammad bin Tughluk, but thought better of it and decided to carry on to Mecca. On his way to Basra he passed through the Strait of Hormuz, where he learned that Abu Sa'id, last ruler of the Ilkhanate Dynasty had died in Persia. Abu Sa'id's territories had subsequently collapsed due to a fierce civil war between the Persians and Mongols.

In 1348, Ibn Battuta arrived in Damascus with the intention of retracing the route of his first hajj. He then learned that his father had died 15 years earlier and death became the dominant theme for the next year or so. The Black Death had struck, and he was on hand as it spread through Syria, Palestine, and Arabia. After reaching Mecca, he decided to return to Morocco, nearly a quarter of a century after leaving home. On the way he made one last detour to Sardinia, then in 1349 returned to Tangier by way of Fez, only to discover that his mother had also died a few months before.

Ibn Battuta visited the Emirate of Granada, which was the final vestige of the Muladi populace in Al-Andalus.

After a few days in Tangier, Ibn Battuta set out for a trip to the Moor controlled territory of al-Andalus on the Iberian Peninsula. King Alfonso XI of Castile and León had threatened to attack Gibraltar, so in 1350 Ibn Battuta joined a group of Muslims leaving Tangier with the intention of defending the port. By the time he arrived, the Black Death had killed Alfonso and the threat of invasion had receded, so he turned the trip into a sight-seeing tour, travelling through Valencia and ending up in Granada.

Following his departure from al-Andalus, he decided to travel through Morocco, one of the few parts of the Muslim world that he had never explored. On his return home, he stopped for a while in Marrakech, which was almost a ghost town following the recent plague and the transfer of the capital to Fez.

Once more Ibn Battuta returned to Tangier, but only stayed for a short while. In 1324, two years before his first visit to Cairo, the West African Malian Mansa, or king of kings, Musa had passed through the same city on his own hajj and caused a sensation with a display of extravagant riches brought from his gold-rich homeland. Although Ibn Battuta never mentioned this visit specifically, when he heard the story it may have planted a seed in his mind as he then decided to cross the Sahara and visit the Muslim kingdoms on its far side.

In the autumn of 1351, Ibn Battuta left Fes and made his way to the town of Sijilmasa on the northern edge of the Sahara in present-day Morocco. There he bought a number of camels and stayed for four months. He set out again with a caravan in February 1352 and after 25 days, arrived at the dry salt-lake bed of Taghaza with its salt mines. All of the local buildings were made from slabs of salt by slaves of the Masufa tribe, who cut the salt in thick slabs for transport by camel. Taghaza was a commercial center and awash with Malian gold, though Ibn Battuta did not form a favourable impression of the place, recording that it was plagued by flies and the water was brackish.

After a ten-day stay in Taghaza, the caravan set out for the oasis of Tasarahla (probably Bir al-Ksaib) where it stopped for three days in preparation for the last and most difficult leg of the journey across the vast desert. From Tasarahla, a Masufa scout was sent ahead to the oasis town of Oualata, where he arranged for water to be transported a distance of four days travel where it would meet the thirsty caravan. Oualata was the southern terminus of the trans-Saharan trade route and had recently become part of the Mali Empire. Altogether, the caravan took two months to cross the 1,600 km (990 mi) of desert from Sijilmasa.

From there, Ibn Battuta travelled southwest along a river he believed to be the Nile (it was actually the river Niger), until he reached the capital of the Mali Empire. There he met Mạnsa Suleyman, king since 1341. Dubious about the miserly hospitality of the king, he nevertheless stayed for eight months. Ibn Battuta disapproved of the fact that female slaves, servants and even the daughters of the sultan went about completely naked. He left the capital in February and journeyed overland by camel to Timbuktu. Though in the next two centuries it would become the most important city in the region, at that time it was a small and growing city there Ibn Battuta was acquainted by a local Malian merchant named Abu Bakr Ibn Yaqub, together they ventured around Timbuktu and sailed to Gao. It was during their travels that Ibn Battuta first encountered the Hippopotamus, which was feared among the local boatmen because it drowned or killed local inhabitants, however Ibn Battuta also mentions an ingenious trick used by locals that allowed them to hunt Hippopotamus for both their flesh and hides. Ibn Battuta is known to have sailed by boat to Gao where he spent a month learning about its inhabitants and geography. While at the oasis of Takedda on his journey back across the desert, he received a message from the Sultan of Morocco commanding him to return home. He set off for Sijilmasa in September 1353 accompanying a large caravan transporting 600 black female slaves and arrived back in Morocco early in 1354.

After returning home from his travels in 1354, and at the instigation of the Sultan of Morocco, Abu Inan Faris, Ibn Battuta dictated an account of his journeys to Ibn Juzayy, a scholar whom he had previously met in Granada. The account is the only source for Ibn Battuta's adventures. The full title of the manuscript may be translated as A Gift to Those Who Contemplate the Wonders of Cities and the Marvels of Travelling but is often simply referred to as the Rihla or "The Journey".

There is no indication that Ibn Battuta made any notes during his twenty-nine year of travels. When he came to dictate an account of them, he had to rely on memory and manuscripts produced by earlier travellers. When describing Damascus, Mecca, Medina and some other places in the Middle East, Ibn Juzayy clearly copied passages from the 12th-century account by Ibn Jubayr. Similarly, most of Ibn Juzayy's descriptions of places in Palestine were copied from an account by the 13th-century traveller Muhammad al-Abdari.

Western Orientalists do not believe that Ibn Battuta visited all the places he described and argue that in order to provide a comprehensive description of places in the Muslim world, he relied on hearsay evidence and made use of accounts by earlier travellers. For example, it is considered very unlikely that Ibn Battuta made a trip up the Volga River from New Sarai to visit Bolghar and there are serious doubts about a number of other journeys such as his trip to Sana'a in Yemen, his journey from Balkh to Bistam in Khorasan and his trip around Anatolia. Some orientalists have also questioned whether he really visited China. Nevertheless, while apparently fictional in places, the Rihla provides an important account of much of the 14th-century world.

Ibn Battuta often experienced culture shock in regions he visited where the local customs of recently converted peoples did not fit in with his orthodox Muslim background. Among the Turks and Mongols, he was astonished at the way women behaved, remarking that on seeing a Turkish couple, and noting the woman's freedom of speech, he had assumed that the man was the woman's servant, but he was in fact her husband. He also felt that dress customs in the Maldives, and some sub-Saharan regions in Africa were too revealing.

After the completion of the Rihla in 1355, little is known about Ibn Battuta's life. He was appointed a judge in Morocco and died in 1368 or 1369.

For centuries his book was obscure, even within the Muslim world, but in the early 19th century extracts were published in German and English based on manuscripts discovered in the Middle East containing abridged versions of Ibn Juzayy's Arabic text. During the French occupation of Algeria in the 1830s, five manuscripts were discovered in Constantine, including two that contained more complete versions of the text. These manuscripts were brought back to the Bibliothèque Nationale in Paris and studied by the French scholars Charles Defrémery and Beniamino Sanguinetti. Beginning in 1853, they published a series of four volumes containing the Arabic text, extensive notes and a translation into French. Defrémery and Sanguinetti's printed text has now been translated into many other languages while Ibn Battuta has grown in reputation and is now a well-known figure.

Last Flight of Amelia Earhart

July 1st, 1937 was a fairly quiet day. A steel strike has just ended in the midwestern United States. Senators and Congressmen called for strict isolationism to avoid being pulled into the conflict that would soon become known as World War II. Jesse Zelda was suing newspaper tycoon William Randolph Hearst for $40,000 claiming that Zelda had been attacked by a "vicious, wild and dangerous ostrich" at the Hearst property in San Simeon. Then the news broke:

Lady lindy lost!

Earhart down in pacific

Earhart disappears

Amelia's plane vanishes

Pacific claims earhart

These headlines heralded the end of the career of one of the most popular and successful aviators of the 20th century and the start of a mystery that would puzzle people for over sixty years: What happened to Amelia Earhart?

Amelia Earhart was born on July 24, 1898 in Atchison, Kansas. Her father was a lawyer and her mother the daughter of a wealthy judge. Her parent's difficult marriage had a profound effect on Amelia Earhart's philosophy of life. Her father, Edwin, was frustrated because he was never able to provide his wife with the kind of lifestyle she had become accustomed to growing up in the judge's house. He gave up his dreams and instead worked as an attorney for the railroad because the position paid the most. Even with this good salary, there were money pressures on Edwin and he began to drink. This lead to an alcohol addiction and the loss of his job.

Edwin moved his family to Des Moines, Iowa, then to St. Paul, Minnesota. His alcoholism continued, though, and he found it difficult to find and keep a job. Finally his wife, Amy, took the children, Amelia and her younger sister, Muriel, to live with friends in Chicago while Edwin went to Kansas City to make a new start.

Amelia saw her father's frustration and unhappiness and determined that she would be an independent woman who could share responsibilities equally with a man and not be dependent on him. She graduated from Chicago's

Hyde Park High School on time in 1916 despite the numerous different schools she'd been moved through. She assisted in a Toronto military hospital during World War I and afterward enrolled in the medical program at Columbia University in New York City in 1919. She did well there, getting A's in Zoology and French and B's in Chemistry and Psychology. One of her professors said, "She had a great curiosity and fine ability to synthesize... who knows what she would have discovered if she had chosen the research laboratory rather than aviation as a career?"

It was not to be, though. Her father was able to open a law office in California and Amelia and her mother moved back in with him. While there, Amelia attended an air show and her father arranged for her to take a trial flight. In the air, Amelia realized she'd found her calling.

She immediately arranged to take lessons on an installment plan from Neta Snook, the first woman graduate of the Curtiss School of Aviation. Later she took additional training from John Montijo, a former Army instructor. In June 1921 Amelia Earhart took her first solo flight.

Earhart soon became a fixture around the airfield in her leather flying jacket, khaki pants, boots and scarf. Her skill increased with her hours in the air and she won grudging respect among the male flyers.

In 1922, with the help of her father, she purchased a sport biplane built by William Kenner. That same year she used her plane to set her first aviation record which was the maximum-altitude-obtained-by-a-woman-pilot: 14,000 feet.

While things were going well for Earhart in the air, her family was having problems back on the ground. Her parents divorced in 1924. Amelia decided to put her aviation on hold, sold her plane and bought a car. She used the car to drive her mother across country to settle in Medfort, Massachusetts where Amelia's sister, Muriel lived. Amelia returned to her studies at Columbia University, but withdrew before the semester was over. Earhart later told friends, "That semester convinced me that I didn't have the qualities to be an M.D. For one, I lacked the patience. I wanted to be doing something, not preparing for it."

In 1926 she accepted a position as a social worker at a settlement house in Boston. She might have made a career in social work if it hadn't been for a phone call two years later from a man named George Palmer Putnam.

In 1919 a U.S. Naval flying boat had crossed the Atlantic to Portugal via the Azores Islands. In 1927 Colonel Charles A. Lindbergh made the first solo flight from New York to Paris. The world was going wild for aviation and Mrs. Frederick Guest of London decided that it was time for a woman to make the cross-Atlantic flight.

Mrs. Guest, who was wealthy, purchased a tri-motor Forkker aircraft and planned to hire a crew to take her on the flight. After reassessing the dangers involved, Mrs. Guest decided to back out and allow another girl "with the right image" to take her place. George Putnam, from the publishing company G.P. Putnam's Sons, who hoped to publish an account of the trip, started searching for a replacement. He hoped to find a girl with a flier's license and an extraordinary amount of courage. He found Amelia Earhart.

Putnam proposed the project to Earhart. She would have liked to have been more than just a passenger on the flight, but realized it would still be a great adventure. Wilmer L. Stultz was selected as the pilot. The Forkker was flown to Trepassey Bay, Newfoundland and there the crew of three waited for good weather. On June 17th, 1928 it cleared and the Forkker, which had been christened Friendship, took off. It landed in Burry Port, Wales with less than an hour of fuel still on board.

The flight brought instant fame to Earhart including a ticker-tape parade through New York City. George Putnam assisted Earhart with her account of the flight published as 20 Hrs., 40 Mins.. After the book was done, she set out on a lecture tour and later took a position as Aviation Editor on Cosmopolitan magazine.

After Putnam's divorce in 1930 he went on a campaign to win Earhart as his wife. He proposed several times before she finally accepted. They were married on February 7th, 1931. George probably wasn't the perfect mate for Earhart but he did provide her a business manager and media spokesman all rolled into one. Most importantly, from Earhart's point of view, Putnam never tried to curtail her freedom to fly.

George arranged for Earhart to promote everything from cigarettes (though she didn't smoke) to pajamas to luggage. She did put the brakes on some of Putnam's plans. When he wanted to sell a small ribbon meant for children and decorated with her signature Earhart told him, "Forget it, George. I won't be a part of cheating youngsters. Adults are supposed to know better, but not kids."

Earhart felt guilty about her fame because she'd only been a passenger on the transatlantic flight, not the pilot. To remedy this on May 20, 1932, exactly five years after Lindbergh, she soloed from Newfoundland to Ireland and became the first woman to fly the Atlantic alone. This earned her audiences with princes, kings and presidents. She became the first woman to be honoured with the Distinguished Flying Cross. Three months later she broke the woman's non-stop transcontinental speed record by flying from Los Angeles, California to Newark, New Jersey, a distance of 2448 miles in 19 hours and five minutes. In 1933 she broke the record again by repeating the trip in 17 hours, 7 minutes and 30 seconds. In 1935 she became the first pilot, man or woman, to solo from Hawaii to California. Three months later she became the first to solo from Los Angeles to Mexico City. Then three weeks later she again soloed from Mexico City to Newark, New Jersey.

Earhart was invited to join Purdue University as a visiting counselor for women students. She loved her role there and the University decided to establish a special fund for aeronautical research. Fifty-thousand dollars was given to Earhart to outfit what she called her "Flying Laboratory": a Lockheed Electra twin-engined airliner. She had the seats removed and extra fuel tanks put in their place. With these changes the plane had a fuel capacity of 1204 gallons which gave it a range of 4,500 miles.

With this new plane Amelia decided it was time to go for one of aviation's most difficult challenges: a flight around the world. A team was quickly put together to support Earhart on her flight. Paul Mantz, an experienced pilot, was hired as technical adviser. Captain Harry Manning and Commander Fred J. Noonan were selected as navigators. Clarence Williams prepared the maps and charts for the flight. It was decided to fly from east to west, so on March 17th, 1937, the Electra took off from Oakland, California heading for Hawaii.

The first leg of the trip went flawlessly and the plane arrived in Honolulu fifteen hours and fifty-two minutes later. The plane refueled and on March 20th it taxied out onto the runway to make the long trip to tiny Howland Island where the U.S. Navy had recently constructed a emergency landing strip. The plane, heavily loaded with fuel, responded sluggishly when Earhart applied the throttle. The plane lurched to the left then swung right. Earhart tried to compensate, but couldn't. The Electra groundlooped, the gear collapsed and a wing was torn open. Fortunately, though fuel poured from ruptured tanks across the ground, there was no fire. Manning, Noonan and Earhart suffered no injuries, but the Electra had to be sent back to Lockheed's facility in Burbank for repairs. It was never clear exactly why the accident happened. Some blamed a blown tire, while Earhart herself believed that the fuel had not been distributed evenly throughout all the tanks causing a weight imbalance.

It took less than two months to repair the plane and a new attempt was scheduled to start on May 20th. Because of the delay, Captain Manning was unable to continue on as navigator and only Noonan flew with Earhart. Seasonal weather conditions prompted them to change the flight to go west to east. The first stop for the Electra (after leaving Oakland) was Tucson Arizona. On June 1st Earhart left U.S. airspace at Miami, Florida on her way to Puerto Rico.

The flight went without major incident for over a month. The plane had small repairs done to it along with several routine engine overhauls as needed. By July 1st they had reached Lae, New Guinea. About seven thousand miles remained to be covered. Most of it was over the wide, empty expanse of the Pacific Ocean. The first leg would take them to Howland Island, a distance of 2556 miles. The plane was loaded almost to capacity with gas. Because Earhart didn't want to dilute her tank of high octane fuel used only on takeoff with the low octane fuel available at Lae, the Electra left 50 gallons short of its 1151 gallon capacity.

The Electra roared down Lae's 3,000 foot runway at 10:30 a.m., July 2nd. The U.S. Coast Guard Cutter Itasca was stationed off of Howland ready to assist by sending a homing signal to Earhart to guide her in. The plane flew overnight and should have approached Howland and the Itasca the next morning, which because the plane was crossing the international dateline, was July 1st.

Picking tiny Howland Island out of the vast Pacific was a difficult navigational problem. To solve it, Noonan had several tools. The first was celestial navigation. By sighting two stars 90 degrees apart from each other on the horizon and then measuring their height above the horizon, Noonan could use a set of prepared tables and a clock to figure his position. If the sky was overcast, and one of Earhart messages from the plane seemed to imply that, Noonan might not have gotten a two-star fix. If this was the case, he could have directed Earhart to fly by "dead reckoning." This navigational method is simple, but prone to error. Noonan would just figure out where the plane was on the map, then use a compass to calculate the course the aircraft should fly to get to the destination. Because compasses are sometimes inaccurate and the distance was long, the Electra could get many miles off course without the crew noticing.

The final method was to home in on the Itasca's radio signal. But, reports from the Electra seemed to indicate it never received a strong enough signal to make that possible.

Even if Noonan couldn't get a star fix, when the sun rose he could use a measurement of its height to figure a line-of-position. This calculation would tell the Electra's crew where they were east-to-west, but not north-to-south. They would have to fly north and south along the right line to find Howland Island. This seems to be precisely what happened. At 7:42 A.M. the Itasca picked up the message, "We must be on you, but we cannot see you. Fuel is running low. Been unable to reach you by radio. We are flying at 1,000 feet." The ship tried to reply, but the plane seemed not to hear. At 8:45 Earhart reported, "We are running north and south." That seems to suggest that for at least an hour Earhart and Noonan were flying along that line-of-position searching for Howland.

Those were the last words heard from the Electra. By that afternoon it was obvious the plane had either gone into the sea, or landed someplace other than Howland. The U.S. Navy started a massive search. Some 262,281 square miles of the Pacific were examined, but no sign of the Electra or its crew was found. Noonan and Earhart were declared dead, and the great mystery of "What happened to Amelia Earhart" began.

In the first few days following the disappearance, there were some 300 reports of messages being received from Earhart's crashed plane. Undoubtedly, most, if not all of them were either hoaxes or misunderstandings.

The conflict that would become World War II was brewing in the Pacific and soon after her disappearance it became a popular idea that she had been captured by the Japanese, or that Japanese forces had shot down her plane, or that she was working with the U.S. government on a secret mission against the Japanese. This story was dramatized in a 1943 film, Flight for Freedom starring Rosalind Russell as a Amelia-Earhart-type flyer. The script followed Earhart's life story precisely, and extended it by suggesting that the disappearance was engineered to allow U.S. Naval forces an excuse to case Japanese military installations.

Shortly after the end of the war Jacqueline Cochran, a pilot and friend of Earhart, traveled to Japan to investigate the role of Japanese women in the hostilities. While there she claimed she'd discovered several files on Earhart which later disappeared. Later, in 1965, retired Air Force Major Joseph Gervias came to the conclusion that Cochran had actually discovered Earhart herself and smuggled her back into the U.S.. There Earhart set up residence in New Jersey under a new name. The woman he named as Earhart denied Gervias' assertions.

In 1960 a woman named Josephine Akiyama came forward with a tale she said took place while she was living on Saipan (a small Pacific island). In 1937 Akiyama had seen two American flyers there, a man and a woman, who were being held by the Japanese. Saipan seems an unlikely candidate as an emergency landing site for the Electra, though, unless Noonan was very, very lost.

Fred Goerner, a CBS broadcaster, took the story seriously and traveled to Siapan, which was at that time under U.S. administration. He found a number of residents who remembered the flyers, though there seemed to be no official record of them. Some reports indicated that the flyers had been executed by the Japanese, something the government of Japan denied. Goerner hired divers to search the bottom of the Siapan harbour and they retrieved what looked like aircraft wreckage. The most interesting piece was what appeared to be an aircraft starter motor and generator. However, careful analysis by the manufacturer proved it was not the one on board the Electra when it left Oakland.

More stories about Siapan emerged including a report from a man stationed on Siapan in 1945. He said he'd been shown graves on Siapan that reportedly belonged to the two mysterious flyers. Another expedition to Siapan recovered the remains of the bodies, but later examination ruled out that they were Earhart or Noonan.

Goerner heard other reports that Earhart's plane may have gone down in the Marshall Islands. The Marshall Islands are much closer to Howland than Siapan. U.S. Naval personnel stationed in the area during World War II reported hearing stories from the Islanders that were very similar to those told on Siapan: Two flyers, a man and a woman, crash landed and were taken captive by the Japanese. No proof emerged from these accounts either, though Goerner finally reached the conclusion that Earhart probably crashed in the Marshall Islands and was later held captive on Siapan.

Investigations into the disappearance of Amelia Earhart and Fred Noonan continue even today. TIGHAR (The International Group for Historic Aircraft Recovery) has an active project trying to determine if the Electra might have gone down on of a collection of islands called the Phoenix Group which lie on the same line-of-position as Howland. If the Electra had missed Howland and turned onto that line heading in a southwardly direction, it might well have reached one of the small islands of Baker, McKean or Gardner (now known as Nikumaroro) and crash landed on it. A search of Nikumaroro turned up aircraft parts similar to those on the Earhart's Electra and a heel from a woman's shoe from the 1930's. Perhaps these items were Earhart's, but there is no proof as of yet. Further expeditions to Nikumaroro are planned.

Somewhere, perhaps on Nikumaroro, perhaps on Siapan, perhaps in the Marshall Islands, maybe at the bottom of the Pacific, is the evidence that will solve the mystery of what happened to Amelia Earhart. Will someone find it? Or will this piece of aviation history remain forever a mystery?

Leonid A. Kulik: Quest for the Answer

The results of even a cursory examination exceeded all the tales of eyewitnesses and my wildest expectations, wrote Leonid Kulik, remembering his first glimpse of the Tunguska destruction. He stood on the bank of the Makirta River at the end of an exhausting journey. As far as he could see upstream and downstream, the riverbank was littered with the trunks of trees uprooted and pushed down in one direction as if smashed by a giant's hand. There was still snow on the ground, and the dead and decaying branches and limbs were outlined in stark relief. Small hills stood out, he later wrote, "picturesquely against the sky and taiga, their almost treeless snow-capped tops stripped bare by the meteorite whirlwind of 1908."

Leonid A. Kulik was born in 1883 in the city of Tartu in Estonia which was later to become part of the Soviet Union. He studied at the St. Petersburg Forestry Institute and later in the Physics and Mathematics Department of Kazan University. He served in the military during the Russo-Japanese War and World War I. Between these two conflicts, he ran afoul of the law and spent a short time in prison for revolutionary activities.

After World War I he taught mineralogy in the city of Tomsk and in 1920 took a position at the Mineralogical Museum in St. Petersburg (later renamed Leningrad).

At the Museum he devoted much of his time to a new discipline: the acquisition and study of meteorites. In 1921 Kulik was charged with the task of locating and examining meteorites that had fallen within the Soviet Union. While preparing for this expedition, he came across an account of an explosion in Tunguska, Siberia, reprinted from an old newspaper:

...a huge meteorite is said to have fallen in Tomsk several sagenes from the railway line near Filimonovo junction and less then 11 versts from Kansk. Its fall was accompanied by a frightful roar and a deafening crash, which was heard more then 40 versts away. The passengers of a train approaching the junction at the time were struck by the unusual noise. The driver stopped the train and the passengers poured out to examine the fallen object, but they were unable to study the meteorite closely because it was red hot...

Strangely enough the story turned out to be wrong in almost every detail, but even so, Kulik had never heard of this impact before and it caused him to go searching for additional old newspaper accounts. By piecing these stories together he determined that the event, which he felt sure was the result of a meteorite fall, must have been enormous. Kulik decided to see if he could find the site during his trip.

During his first expedition Kulik only managed to figure out the general location of the blast area, not actually visit it. Afterward Kulik continued to collect stories about the event.

A geologist sent this account which was told to him by a local herdsman: "Fifteen years ago his brother, who was a Tungus and could speak little Russian, lived on the River Chamb'e. One day a terrible explosion occurred, the force of which was so great that the forest was flattened for many versts along both banks of the River Chamb'e. His brother's hut was flattened to the ground, its roof was carried away by the wind, and most of his reindeer fled in fright. The noise deafened his brother and the shock caused him to suffer a long illness..."

Entnographer I. M. Suslov interviewed the family who had been sleeping twenty-five miles southeast of the blast site when the event occurred. The entire group was thrown down by the force of the blast and several knocked unconscious. The wife reported that when they awoke they found "...the forest blazing around them with many fallen trees. There was also a great noise." Some of the children described "A terrible storm," Suslov continued, "So great it was difficult to stand upright in it, [that] blew down the trees near their hut."

Despite resistance from some of his colleagues who questioned the value of a trip based on rumours told by backwoods peasents, Kulik used these and other reports to convince the Academy of Sciences to fund a second expedition.

The 1927 expedition had been planned for the spring. This would mean they would reach the area before the ground in the region became a swamp and the mosquitoes intolerable. Even taking these precautions the journey was difficult going since Kulik was still not sure of where the exact blast site was and the maps they were using were inaccurate.

The first leg of their trip was accomplished by using the Trans-Siberian railway. Kulik and a research assistant travelled from Leningrad to the remote station of Taishet. From there they used horse drawn sleds to make their way up the Angara River to Keshma, a small village where they purchased more supplies.

From that point on the way grew ever more difficult. The land became more rugged. Deep gulches and steep hillsides blocked their path. Their compasses became confused by the high latitude. It took until the end of March to reach the tiny village of Vanavara located on the Stony Tunguska River. Vanavara was the last outpost of civilization before the expedition plunged into the primitive forest-swamp where Kulik was sure the meteorite had fallen.

In the village Kulik hired a guide named Ilya Potapovich and started interviewing locals about what they remembered about the blast. He found that many of the local people did not like to discuss the event. They believed that the fiery body that had fallen was a visitation of the god Ogdy. Ogdy had cursed the area by smashing trees and killing the animals. No man now approached the site for fear of being cursed by the god.

This story only peaked Kulik's interest and he soon set out on horseback, with the guide, to find the fall. An unusually heavy snow blocked their path, though, and they were forced to return to the village and await better weather.

On April 18 the expedition set out again with pack horses. This time they followed the course of the river. They took three days to reach the hut of Okhchen, a friendly herdsman, located on the Chamb'e river. By that time both Kulik and his assistant were suffering from infections and lack of proper food. Only the belief that their destination was only a short distance away kept them going.

They left the horses at Okhchen's home and loaded their supplies onto reindeer for the last portion of the journey. After two days of following the bank of the Chamb'e due north they came to the Makirta river and saw the first evidence of the Tunguska blast. The already exhausted party marched northward into the devastation, sometimes having to hack their way through the dead entangled limbs and branches of the fallen trees. As they travelled closer to the center of the area Kulik noticed that the trees had been burned from above. He was sure it was the work of a sudden flash of intense heat, not a forest fire. The scientist speculated that what the meteorite had "pushed ahead of it was doubtless a giant bubble of superheated atmosphere, hotter than the blast of any earthly furnace..."

They travelled for two more days through the destruction when suddenly his guides, Potapovich and Okhchen, apparently fearful of Ogdy's punishment, refused to go forward. Kulik was forced to return to Vanavara and hire new guides.

On April 30th, Kulik, with his new helpers, set out again for the fall site. This time the party, aware of the difficulty of marching through the forest, built rafts to carry them along the Chamb'e and Khushmo rivers toward their destination. The water courses were swollen with the spring melt and it was necessary to navigate several rapids.

It had been three months since the expedition had left Leningrad. No word had come back from Kulik, and his colleagues began to fear the worst. Was the scientist lost or dead in the uncharted Siberian wilderness? Or had he simply not sent word back because he was embarrassed about finding nothing?

Back in the field the expedition had gone as far as they could by water and headed north on foot finally reaching the ruined forest on May 20th. For a week they cut though the tangle of dead tree limbs and marched toward the center of the fallen wood. Kulik finally set up camp near the mouth of the Churgima River believing that the crater he sought must be just beyond the next ridge in a marshy basin his guides referred to as the Southern Swamp.

From this camp Kulik made daily trips out across the dead forest until he circled the entire area. From his observations he could see that on every side of the swamp the fallen trees lay with their tops pointing outward. That meant that the center of the swamp was the fall point of the meteorite for which he was searching. Instead of finding a giant crater, though, Kulik saw a standing forest of what looked like telephone poles. Each trunk stood straight and tall, but charred and stripped of its branches.

In the very center of this forest Kulik found a peat marsh blasted and tortured into a fantastic landscape. "The solid ground," wrote Kulik, "heaved outward from the spot in giant waves, like waves in water." He also found dozens of "peculiar flat holes" ranging in size from ten feet to fifty feet in diameter. Each was several yards deep.

Kulik carefully documented and photographed the area and decided to return on a later expedition and probe the holes with digging equipment in an attempt to locate fragments of the meteorite he thought might be beneath them.

Realizing that nothing more could be done on this trip and that the group had only three or four days of food left, Kulik decided to leave. It was a good decision. The summer thaws soon made travelling increasingly dangerous. The expedition set out and after nine days, having supplemented their diet with ducks, fish and local plants, they arrived back in Vanavara at the end of June.

Kulik returned to the Academy with enough photographs and documentation to convince even his most skeptical colleagues that something amazing had happened along the Tunguska river. He led two more expeditions back to Siberia, one in 1929 and another in 1938, but was never able to establish that the culprit in the blast was a meteorite. Even today the exact cause of the explosion is unknown.

Kulik continued to work on the problem until, while fighting for his country in World War II, he was captured and died of typhus in a Nazi prison camp on April 24th, 1942.

The success of Kulik's expedition wasn't in solving the mystery of the Siberian blast of 1908, but in proving to the world that objects have, and continue, to fall from space and can have a devastating result on Earth. This knowledge has led to a better understanding of how these impact events effect life on our planet and how they might explain such mysteries as the death of the dinosaurs.

Howard Carter and the "Curse of the Mummy"

Death Shall Come on Swift Wings to Him Who Disturbs the Peace of the King... – Supposedly engraved on the exterior of King Tutankhamen's Tomb

The king was only nineteen when he died, perhaps murdered by his enemies. His tomb, in comparison with his contemporaries, was modest. After his death, his successors made an attempt to expunge his memory by removing his name from all the official records. Even those carved in stone. As it turns out, his enemy's efforts only ensured his eventual fame. His name was Tutankhamen: King Tut.

The ancient Egyptians revered their Pharaohs as Gods. Upon their deaths the King's bodies were carefully

preserved by embalming. The mummified corpses were interned in elaborate tombs (like the Great Pyramid) and surrounded with all the riches the royals would need in the next life. The tombs were then carefully sealed. Egypt's best architects designed the structures to resist thieves. In some cases heavy, hard-granite plugs were used to block passageways. In others, false doorways and hidden rooms were designed to fool intruders. Finally, in a few cases, a curse was placed on the entrance.

Most of these precautions failed. In ancient times grave robbers found their way into the tombs. They unsealed the doors, chiseled their way around the plugs and found the secrets of the hidden rooms. They stripped the dead Kings of their valuables. We will never know if any of the thieves suffered the wrath of a curse.

Archaeologists from Europe became very interested in Egypt in the 19th century. They uncovered the old tombs and explored their deep recesses always hoping to find that one forgotten crypt that had not been plundered in antiquity. They knew that the Pharaohs had been buried with untold treasures that would be of immense artistic, scientific, and monetary value. Always the archaeologists were disappointed.

In 1891 a young Englishman named Howard Carter arrived in Egypt. Over the years he became convinced that there was at least one undiscovered tomb. That of the almost unknown King Tutankhamen. Carter found a backer for his tomb search in the wealthy Lord Carnarvon. For five years Carter dug looking for the missing Pharaoh and found nothing.

Carnarvon summonded Carter to England in1922 to tell him he was was calling off the search. Carter managed to talk the lord into supporting him for one more season of digging. Returning to Egypt the archaeologist brought with him a yellow canary.

"A golden bird!" Carter's foreman, Reis Ahmed, exclaimed. "It will lead us to the tomb!"

Perhaps it did. On November 4th, 1922 Carter's workmen discovered a step cut into the rock that had been hidden by debris left over from the building of the tomb of Ramesses IV. Digging further they found fifteen more leading to an ancient doorway that appeared to be still sealed. On the doorway was the name Tutankhamen.

When Carter arrived home that night his servant met him at the door. In his hand he clutched a few yellow feathers. His eyes large with fear, he reported that the canary had been killed by a cobra. Carter, a practical man, told the servant to make sure the snake was out of the house. The man grabbed Carter by the sleeve.

"The pharaoh's serpent ate the bird because it led us to the hidden tomb! You must not disturb the tomb!"

Scoffing at such superstitious nonsense, Carter sent the man home.

Carter immediately sent a telegram to Carnarvon in England and waited anxiously for his arrival. Carnarvon made it to Egypt by November 26th and watched as Carter made a hole in the door. Carter leaned in, holding a candle, to take a look. Behind him Lord Carnarvon asked, "Can you see anything?"

Carter answered, "Yes, wonderful things."

The day the tomb was opened was one of joy and celebration for all those involved. Nobody seemed to be concerned about any curse. Rumours later circulated that Carter had found a tablet with the curse inscribed on it, but hid it immediately so it would not alarm his workers. Carter denied doing so.

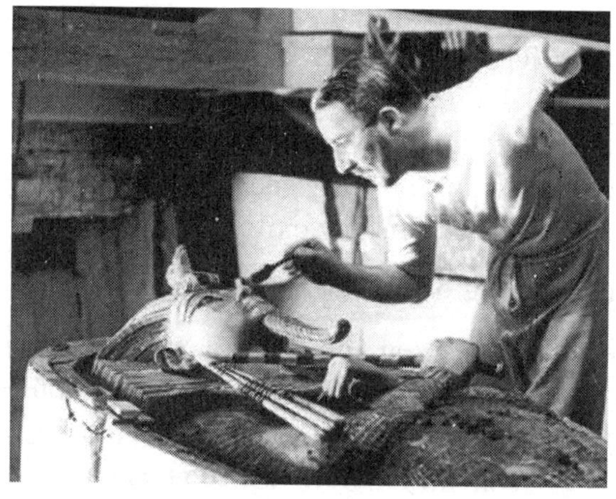

The tomb was intact and contained an amazing collection of treasures including a stone sarcophagus. The sarcophagus contained three gold coffins nested within each other. Inside the final one was the mummy of the boy-king, Pharaoh Tutankhamen.

A few months after the tomb's opening tragedy struck. Lord Carnarvon, 57, was taken ill and rushed to Cairo. He died a few days later. The exact cause of death was not known, but it seemed to be from an infection started by an insect bite. Legend has it that when he died there was a short power failure and all the lights throughout Cairo went out. His son reported that back on his estate in England his favourite dog howled and suddenly dropped dead.

Even more strange, when the mummy of Tutankhamun was unwrapped in 1925, it was found to have a wound on the left cheek in the same exact position as the insect bite on Carnarvon that lead to his death.

By 1929 eleven people connected with the discovery of the Tomb had died early and of unnatural causes. This included two of Carnarvon's relatives, Carter's personal secretary, Richard Bethell, and Bethell's father, Lord Westbury. Westbury killed himself by jumping from a building. He left a note that read, "I really cannot stand any more horrors and hardly see what good I am going to do here, so I am making my exit."

What horrors did Westbury refer to?

The press followed the deaths carefully attributing each new one to the "Mummy's Curse". By 1935 they had credited 21 victims to King Tut. Was there really a curse? Or was it all just the ravings of a sensational press?

Herbert E. Winlock, the director of the Metropolitan Museum of Art in New York City, made his own calculations about the effectiveness of the curse. According to Winlock's figures of the 22 people present when the tomb was opened in 1922, only 6 had died by 1934. Of the 22 people present at the opening of the sarcophagus in 1924, only 2 died in the following ten years. Also ten people were there when the mummy was unwrapped in 1925, and all survived until at least 1934.

In 2002 a medicine scholar at Monash University in Melbourne, Australia, named Mark Nelson, completed a study which purportedly showed that the curse of King Tut never really existed. Nelson selected 44 Westerners in Egypt at the time the tomb was discovered. Of those, twenty-five of the group were people potentially exposed to the curse either because they were at the breaking of the sacred seals in the tomb, or at the opening of the sarcophagus, or at the opening of the coffins, or the unwrapping of the mummy. The study showed that these exposures had no effect on the length of their survival when compared to those not exposed.

Perhaps, the power of a curse is in the mind of the person who believes in it. Howard Carter, the man who actually opened the tomb, never believed in the curse and lived to a reasonably old age of 66 before dying of entirely natural causes.

Several people have suggested that illnesses associated with the ancient Egyptian tombs may have a rational explanation based in biology. Dr. Ezzeddin Taha, of Cairo University, examined the health records of museum workers and noticed that many of them had been exposed to Aspergillus niger, a fungus that causes fever, fatigue and rashes. He suggested that the fungus might have been able to survive in the tombs for thousands of years and then was picked up by archaeologists when they entered.

Dr. Nicola Di Paolo, an Italian physician identified another possible fungus, Aspergillus ochraceus, at Egyptian archaeological sites suggesting it might also have made visitors to the tomb, or even those that just handled artifacts from the tombs, sick. Aspergillus ochraceus has not been shown to be fatal, however.

In 1999 a German microbiologist, Gotthard Kramer, from the University of Leipzig, analyzed 40 mummies and identified several potentially dangerous mold spores on each. Mold spores are tough and can survive thousands of years even in a dark, dry tomb. Although most are harmless, a few can be toxic.

Kramer thinks that when tombs were first opened and fresh air gusted inside, these spores could have been blown up into the air. "When spores enter the body through the nose, mouth or eye mucous membranes," he adds, "they can lead to organ failure or even death, particularly in individuals with weakened immune systems."

For this reason archaeologists now wear protective gear (such as masks and gloves) when unwrapping a mummy, something explorers from the days of Howard Carter and Lord Carnarvon didn't do.

So was the curse of the mummy a mold spore named Aspergillus flavus or Cephalosporium? Or was it all media hype? Or is there another explanation?

Dian Fossey and the Gorillas of the Virunga Volcanoes

Another bothersome tourist, Dr. Louis Leakey grumbled to himself. The American woman wanted to tour Dr. Leakey's excavation at Olduvia. Leakey was by then one of the most well-known paleoanthropologists in the world. In 1959, with his wife, Mary, he'd discovered the remains of Zinjanthropus, and a year later Homo habilis, both thought to be early relatives of human beings. By 1963 he was much too busy to be giving tours of his digs, even to the tall, attractive American woman with the dark hair.

Still, Leakey obliged, charging the woman 14 shillings to look around. He had just uncovered an important giraffe fossil. In her enthusiasm to look at it, the woman slipped coming down a steep slope, fell into the excavation, sprained her ankle and damaged the valuable specimen. For good measure, the pain from the ankle made the woman vomit on the fossil. This is how Louis Leakey came to meet Dian Fossey.

Dian Fossey was born in 1932. Her childhood was difficult. She was the only child of George and Kitty Fossey. Her father drank heavily, causing a divorce when Dian was only three. She saw little of him afterwards. When Dian was five her mother married Richard Price. Price did not treat his new step-daughter well. He had her eat dinner in the kitchen with the housekeeper until she was ten. When she went to college, he financed little of her education.

Dian Fossey was trained as an occupational therapist and found a job at the Kosair Children's Hospital in Kentucky. She seemed to be able to communicate with the disabled children in ways others could not. Though she loved her job, she had a desire to see more of the world, so she borrowed against her next three-years earnings to finance a trip to Africa. Of particular interest to her was the excavations at Olduvia and the mountain gorillas of the Virunga Volcanoes of Central Africa.

The Mountain Gorilla (Gorilla Gorilla Beringe) was unknown until 1902 when a German, Captain von Beringe, observed some tall "man-like" apes in what is now modern Rwanda. Little was known about them until naturalist George Schaller spent a year studying the animals in 1959-1960. Schaller's book, *The Year of the Gorilla*, changed the notion of the largest of apes from "King Kong monsters" to "amiable vegetarians" that lived in small, cohesive family groups.

Even after injuring her ankle, Fossey was determined to go on with her plans to see the great apes of the Virunga. Mary Leakey bandaged her up and Fossey headed off to the mountains. Two weeks later, she staggered up a 10,000-foot volcano and got the first glimpse of the gentle giants that were to occupy most of her life.

"Peeking through the vegetation, we could distinguish an equally curious phallax of black, leather-countenanced, furry-headed primates peering back at us," Fossey wrote later in her book *Gorillas in the Mist*. "Their bright eyes darted nervously from under heavy brows as though trying to identify us as familiar friends or possible foes. Immediately I was struck by the physical magnificence of the huge jet-black bodies blended against the green palette wash of the thick forest foliage."

Fossey returned to Kentucky where she wrote several articles for the Louisville Courier-Journal about her experiences with the gorillas of the Virunga. In 1966 when Louis Leakey stopped at Louisville on a speaking tour, he met with Fossey again. Leakey told Fossey that he believed long-term studies of the great apes were an important key to understanding the behaviour of the primate fossils he'd been digging up. Towards this end he had talked Jane Goodall into studying the chimpanzees of Gombe several years before. Now he was looking for someone to take on a long-term study of the Mountain Gorillas. Would Dian be interested?

Fossey had no formal training in studying animal behaviour. However, Leakey was less interested in her academic credentials than in her determination to see the job through until the end. Fossey had determination to spare. After she agreed to do the study on the gorillas, Leakey told her that he would secure the necessary funding. He also suggested, jokingly, that she have her appendix removed as a precaution since she would be working so far away from medical help. Later Leakey sent a letter to tell her he wasn't serious about her appendix, but it was too late. Fossey had already undergone the surgery.

Against her parents wishes, Fossey left for Africa in late 1966. She spent the first few days with Jane Goodall at Gombe to study her methods, then went to Nairobi where Leakey helped her obtain the supplies for her jungle camp. This included two tents and a used LandRover that was christened with the name "Lily."

Experienced field photographer Alan Root agreed to accompany her to her Congo base and assist in setting up camp. While he was still there, she attempted to follow a gorilla trail through the forest. After tracing it for five minutes she was surprised to find that Root was no longer with her. Returning to where she'd picked up the trail, she found Root waiting for her. "Dian," he said, "if you are ever going to contact gorillas, you must follow their tracks to where they are going, rather than backtrack trails to where they've been."

Root stayed with Fossey for two days. When he left, Fossey later wrote, "I clung on to my tent pole simply to avoid running after him."

The jungles that line the hills of the Virunga Volcanoes are cold, dark and muddy. The region is shared by the countries of Rwanda, Uganda and the Congo. Over 67 inches of rain fall each year in those mountains. Storms that produce hail stones large enough to dent tin roofs are frequent. The 45-degree slopes are tangled with thick vegetation including nettles that deliver a painful sting even through multiple layers of clothing.

Conditions were extra difficult for Fossey. She had been an asthmatic child and she smoked. The thin air at the 10,000-foot elevation of her camp often left her gasping for breath. Those first few days on the mountain were intensely lonely for Fossey. The only two other human beings there were her two African employees whose language she did not speak (Soon after the camp was set up, she thought her cook was announcing plans to murder her, when he was only inquiring if she wanted some hot water).

Her determination saw her through, however, and she was soon at work tracking the great apes. First, she adopted the strategy of sneaking up silently on them and quietly observing. Later, though, she changed her approach by announcing her presence to the gorillas by imitating their sounds. After six months she was able to approach some of the groups as close as thirty feet.

Then one day her research came to a sudden end. The rebel leader Moise Tshombe took control of the Kisangani and Bukavu regions and the eastern end of the Congo came under threat. The park director sent soldiers up the mountain to Fossey's camp with orders for her to leave.

Fossey packed up her Landrover and after being detained for several weeks, headed for the border. Though she was scared, she managed to make it out of the country through a closed border by bribing the guards. Even though the episode had been frightening, within two weeks she was preparing to return to the Virunga Volcanoes.

This time she placed her camp on the Rwandan side of the mountains, but only five miles from the border through which she had so recently escaped. Leakey was criticized for letting her return after such a close call, but wrote to Fossey, "If people like you and me and Jane and others, whose work takes them into strange places, put our personal safety first we would never get any work done at all."

It took a long time for Fossey to get the Rwandan gorillas used to her presence. The animals in the Congo had known George Schaller and accepted him coming close to them. In Rwanda the animals were more wary. Fossey carefully eased her way into their lives, approaching them on hands and knees and trying to say in gorilla etiquette "I am here and I am harmless." This worked well, but took time. Pushing the gorillas too hard could cause them to respond in fear.

Once Bob Campbell, a National Geographic photographer, suggested that Fossey sneak up on a group of gorillas so that he could get a picture of them with Fossey in the frame. She came within forty feet of them when the leader of the group, who Fossey had named Rafiki, charged at her. Four other gorillas followed. They charged and screamed at Fossey in a terrifying display for half an hour as she sat with her back to them, pretending to feed. The noise was deafening. Eventually the group moved off, but Fossey was shocked that a group of gorillas that had been so friendly to her could so quickly change.

As time went on Fossey began to find just the right mix of aggressiveness and aversion necessary to get close to the animals without frightening them. As she was sitting among them one day, a young male she'd named Peanuts came over and touched her. Campbell caught the encounter on film and later said the experience for Fossey was "almost overwhelming."

After that it was difficult for Fossey to just be a dispassionate academic observer. Several of the gorillas got used to being in very close contact with her. An adult female named Macho would come over and gaze into Fossey's eyes. Digit, a young male, and Fossey's favourite, would play with her hair or gently whack her with leaves. She wrote Leakey, "I just about burst open with happiness every time I get within 1 or 2 feet of them."

Fossey left her gorillas in 1970 to enroll in Cambridge and get her academic credentials. She didn't like it there. "I hate it here because it isn't Africa," she wrote to Leakey after the first semester. She stuck it out though because she realized that getting her Ph.D. was key to receiving the grants necessary to continue her gorilla studies in the field.

The life of mountain gorillas was recorded in detail by Fossey. The group is usually a tightly-knit family consisting of an adult male leader, his adult brother, or nephew, and a few adult females and their children. They move and feed together, rarely separated by more then a hundred feet. The children are treated very tenderly by even the largest of males. The adult males are often referred to as "silverbacks" because the fur on the back turns gray as they grow older.

Gorilla families rarely interact with other neighbouring groups except to occasionally transfer maturing females back and forth. Sometimes the exchange is not voluntary. A silverback may "raid" a neighbouring family to obtain females.

Fossey was moved to name the lead silverback in one group "Uncle Bert" after beloved uncle Albert Chapin. Chapin was one of the few adults, along with his wife, who had really cared for Fossey when she was young. Perhaps Fossey found in this family of shy, gentle primates a tenderness and cohesion that she had never known herself while she was growing up.

Her close relationship with the animals can be illustrated in an incident in 1976. Fossey was depressed. She had been spending less and less time in the field and more time back at her camp doing paperwork. This was partly because she now had graduate students working for her to observe the animals, but mostly because her health was failing. Her legs were weak and she had hairline fractures on her feet that made walking to have daily contact with the animals impossible.

Even so, one day she ventured out to find them. They were huddled together against the rain. She decided not to get too close, fearing that her interaction with them might make them less wary of poachers. Sitting there watching them she felt cold and alone in the dark, misty jungle.

Suddenly a comforting arm encircled her. She looked up to see Digit's warm, gentle, brown eyes. He patted her head, and they sat side by side cuddling against the rain.

Though animals of the Virunga Volcanoes were protected by national parks, poaching became an increasing problem as time went on. Fossey was constantly clearing snares and traps from the area. While most of the traps were set with the intention of capturing antelope for food, they would occasionally ensnare gorillas.

Fossey learned to hate poaching when she found a bull buffalo caught in the trunk of a tree. It was bellowing in pain. Poachers had discovered the trapped creature and, while it was still living, hacked off its hind legs for the meat. Fossey was in tears as she shot the beast to put it out of its misery. Fossey loved animals of every type, but unfortunately she lived in a land where animals were valued mostly as food or skins.

The poachers soon learned that there was money to be made by selling to Westerners gorilla heads and hands for trophies. More money could be made by supplying zoos with gorilla babies for exhibition. This last activity was especially damaging to the gorillas populations. Gorillas families would fight to the death to protect their young and often a whole group would be destroyed to obtain one youngster.

When Fossey arrived in Africa in 1966 there had been an estimated 480 mountain gorillas left in the park. Poaching and encroachment were slowly causing their numbers to dwindle. She felt that unless something was done, the animals would face extinction very soon. She was terrified for her gorillas.

Her fear was justified. On New Years Day, 1978, they found the body of Digit. He had died defending his family against poachers. His killers had hacked off his hands and head. Six months later, the ape she had named Uncle Bert, was also killed. Poachers got several other members of Bert's group too. Fossey buried the bodies in a cemetery she built by her camp.

After this Fossey declared war on the poachers. She organized anti-poaching patrols and placed bounties on poachers heads. She killed their cattle if it strayed onto park land. She burned their houses. She began to require her students to carry guns. She called this "active conservation," but others began to claim that what Fossey was running was a war rather than a research camp. The truth was that she was running a war. Dian Fossey and the gorillas against the poachers.

Fossey began to circulate stories that she was a sorceress who could curse her enemies. There were rumours she tortured poachers if she caught them. Meanwhile, people in the West began to wonder if she was insane.

The tension around her camp became so high that Fossey was forced to leave Rwanda in 1981 not to return until 1983. Despite this cooling off period, Fossey was found murdered in her cabin on December 26th, 1985. She was buried in the cemetery next to her beloved gorillas. Her killer, probably a poacher, was never found.

Was Fossey right to take the anti-poaching campaign into her own hands? Her critics argue that she was too close to the gorillas, too emotionally involved with them to be a good conservationist. Certainly the gorilla population is under threat even today, though a lucrative program of gorilla tourism has done much in recent years to improve Rwanda's policy toward the great apes' conservation.

One thing is certain, however. As it says on the marker at Dian Fossey's grave:

Dian Fossey 1932-1985

No one loved gorillas more...

Raiders of the Last Tomb

At midnight, on February 25th, 1987, Dr. Walter Alva, Director of the Bruning Museum, in Peru, was awakened by a phone call. On the other end of the line was the Peruvian Investigative Police (PIP) from the city of Chiclayo. The chief of police wanted Alva to come and examine a sack full of what they believed to be artifacts stolen from a local archaeological site: the smallest of an eroded and ancient set of three pyramids called Huaca Rajada.

Alva, sick with bronchitis for three days, was at first reluctant to make the drive to the station. The Police often detained suspected antiquities thieves, or huaqueros as they were called, with little reason. Undoubtedly, Alva thought, the items the police had seized were of minor importance and not worth a midnight ride. Still, the chief was insistent and Alva finally agreed to go.

By the time he arrived at the PIP station the archaeologist was sure the whole thing was a hoax. The police had been told that the artifacts came from an ancient tomb of a mysterious people known as the Moche that lived on was is now the north coast of Peru between 100 BC and 700 AD. Alva knew that the Huaca Rajada pyramids were of Chimu origin. The Chimu civilizaion came after the Moche.

The police chief handed Alva a package which he opened. The archaeologist was shocked. He had expected a piece of pottery. Inside was a human mask made of hammered gold. The eyes were of silver and had pupils made of rare cobalt blue stones. Even more surprising than the object itself was its origin. The style was definitely Moche. Alva and many other archaeologists had been wrong about the pyramids.

The raiding of the site at Huaca Rajada had started several weeks before. A local 36 year-old huaqueros named Ernil Bernal had led a small group of looters to the pyramids. Jobs in the village of Sipan, near the pyramids were scarce and the poverty oppressive. For generations the huaqueros had been looting archaeological locations hoping to find a few gold beads or rare ceramics to sell. That night at Huaca Rajada Ernil and his crew hit the jackpot.

They had tunneled into the pyramid for some distance, but not found anything of value. Then Ernil noticed that the tunnel roof looked strange, as if it had been patched. Taking a long rod he jammed it into the patch to find out what was behind it. Unexpectedly the ceiling collapsed and Ernil was buried in a cave-in. When his brother came to his rescue he found Ernil up to his neck in material from a hidden chamber above: the looter was covered with a king's ransom of gold, silver and precious stones. They had found the crypt of an ancient Moche Lord.

The raiders packed up the treasure-trove in sacks. Before they even left the tunnels, though, the thieves turned against each other and one was shot dead. Another, deprived of his share of the loot, ran to the police. Several days later the police raided Ernil's house finding the death mask and several other smaller items. Most of the treasure was already on its way through the underground market to illegal private collections and museums in the United States and around the world. It was the leftovers found at the house that had been shown to Dr. Alva.

The police drove Dr. Alva out to Huaca Rajada. The pyramids were now swarming with huaqueros drawn by the stories of treasure. It took bursts of automatic gunfire in the air to scare them off.

Dr. Alva now had a choice to make. Common sense argued that he should just fill up the tunnels and hope no more damage would be done to the pyramid until a full excavation could be organized and funded someday in some distant future. Or, Alva could start excavation immediately. If he made the second choice he would have to proceed with no money, little police support and no official permission.

The archaeologist knew the pyramid might contain more Moche burial chambers. If it did they were probably filled with artifacts that would finally unlock the mystery of the ancient Moche people. If the looters came back and raided the tombs, the secrets only a careful scientific excavation would yield would be gone forever. Alva decided to start digging.

Tensions were high at Huaca Rajada when the excavation began. The original looter, Ernil Bernal, had been killed in a confrontation with police. The villagers from Sipan grew increasingly hostile toward Alva. Many of them viewed the artifacts as an inheritance from their ancestors that belonged to them, not the archaeologist or his museum.

Alva managed to get some money together and hire a few of the villagers to help in the excavation, but the police could only spare two men to stand guard. The archaeologist proceeded carefully with the dig, slowly peeling off layer after layer of brick, soil and sand. Then they found a body. From the trappings buried with the man, he appeared to be a Moche warrior. Alva wondered if he had been interned there to "guard" something further down.

After removing the body they continued digging and soon came to the rotting roof of what had been a chamber. Sand and soil sifting through the ceiling had long ago filled the room. Alva's crew dug slowly through the chamber until they found a box with copper straps: a lord's coffin. They had found a royal Moche tomb that had never been opened.

The coffin contained the body of a Moche Lord along with his burial treasures which included a one-pound crescent-shaped headdress of hammered gold, a gold death mask, and a necklace composed of sixteen gold discs. The find was of incalculable importance.

Outside the site, which now looked like an armed camp, the villagers gathered and shouted that they wanted their "ancestor's inheritance." The police, in fear, launched tear gas. Tension mounted even more. No help was coming and it seemed as if Alva's men could hold out only one more night before those gathered around the pyramid would overrun it, assaulting the digging crew, and plundering the royal tomb.

The next morning Dr. Alva went to the edge of the dig and confronted one of the leaders of those gathered outside, a man named Alberto Jaime. He told Jaime that his "inheritance" was waiting on the top of the pyramid and he should go and get it before anybody stole it from him. Then Alva clipped the barb wire fence around the dig, grabbed Jaime by the collar and dragged him to the excavated tomb. In astonishment the rest of the villagers followed. Alva thrust a shovel into Jaime's hands and dared him to steal from his ancestors and sack "his father's sacred tomb." Jaime, speechless, did nothing.

Dr. Alva then turned to the villagers and told them that once a great King of the Moche civilization had made his headquarters in their village. When the king died his people dressed him in gold. "Nothing less was good enough for the exalted Lord of Sipan," Alva explained.

The villagers suddenly saw the tomb not as a vault of gold, but the shrine of an esteemed ancestor. From that point on the tomb was secure. Not just a few archaeologists experienced the wonder of the discovery, but thousands of visitors made the pilgrimage to see the "magic" of the Moche Lord who had been entombed in a golden uniform.

Before the excavation of Huaca Rajada was over, the tomb of another Lord of Sipan, and a tomb of a High Priest were discovered in the pyramid. Much was learned about these mysterious ancient people who were capable of creating beautiful ceramic and gold artwork, but also were capable of harsh, ritualized violence. Much of the artwork found depicted the Moche human sacrifice ceremony.

The pyramid is now a tourist attraction that has boosted the economy of Sipan. As for Alberto Jaime, the leader of the mob that almost plundered the tomb, he now works as a tour guide.

In Search for the Treasure of Troy

Heinrich Schliemann was not the most famous archaeologist of his day, though he was famous. Neither was he the most skilled. He rarely followed good archaeological procedures at his excavations and was roundly criticized by later archaeologists. He wasn't even the most scrupulous of those in his profession, something confirmed by his illegal smuggling of a priceless historic treasure out of the country of Turkey.

He was, however, perhaps the luckiest archaeologist of all time. His life was a rags-to-riches story capped by the discovery of not one, but two treasures and a lost city that most reputable archaeologists of his day thought was only a myth.

Heinrich was born in 1822 in Beubuckow, Germany, the son of a Protestant pastor. His father scorned the usual children's fairy tales and instead told little Heinrich the classics of literature which he translated into simple language. One of the boy's favourite stories was Homer's Iliad: the story of Paris of the City of Troy who kidnaped the beautiful Helen from her Greek husband, King Menelaus, and the resulting war between the Greeks and the Trojans to get her back. A war that ended, according to Homer, when the Greeks used a wooden horse filled with soldiers to capture the city.

Little Heinrich decided that when he grew up he would go and look for the city of Troy and its treasure. None of his playmates shared his enthusiasm for this project except Minna Meincke, daughter of a farmer that lived nearby. Schliemann later wrote, "Minna entered into all my vast plans for the future. Thus a warm attachment grew up between us. In our childish simplicity we exchanged vows of eternal love."

At age nine they made plans. They would marry when grown, excavate the nearby castle that supposedly had belonged to the famous robber baron, Henning Von Holstein, find his hidden treasure and then use the treasure to sail to Asia Minor and excavate the treasure of Troy.

Alas, it was not to be. Pastor Schliemann's family had a falling out with the rest of the community and Heinrick was forbidden to see his young friend. "I have undergone many troubles in different parts of the world, but none of them ever caused me a thousandth part of the grief I felt at the age of nine years for my separation from my little bride," wrote Schliemann later.

At fourteen Schliemann was apprenticed to a local grocer. When he hurt his back and could no longer lift heavy weights, he moved to Hamburg. Unable to hold a job there because of his injury, he signed on as a cabin boy on a ship. The ship went down during a bad storm off the coast of Holland. Finding his way to Amsterdam he got a poorly-paying job.

Schliemann might have stayed in that position for life if he hadn't discovered his knack of learning languages. He taught himself English, Dutch and French. Later he learned Spanish, Portuguese, and Italian. The knowledge of these languages enabled him to find a good position in an import/export firm. He learned Russian and moved to the company's branch office in St. Petersburg in 1846. While there he increased this employer's business while making a small fortune for himself trading in indigo dye.

Now on his way to success, Schliemann wrote to a friend in Germany and had him pass on a marriage proposal to his childhood sweetheart. He was broken-hearted upon learning she had married someone else a month earlier.

Schliemann travelled to California to inherit a fortune made by his brother in the 1849 gold rush. When he arrived there he discovered that the money was gone, but Schliemann managed to double his own funds through the gold dust trade. Schliemann became a naturalized U.S. citizen, but returned to Russian in 1852. He married there, but it didn't work out.

Business was still good, though, and in 1863, at age forty-one, Schliemann retired a millionaire. This permitted him to travel, and he visited the island of Ithaca and Mycenae, the homes of Odysseus and Agamemnon, two of the kings who had fought in the Trojan war. Then he crossed the sea to Turkey to look for the city of Troy itself.

Most historians and archaeologists of the time believed that there never had been a real city of Troy. Of the few that did, most pointed to a hill named Bunarbashi located a few miles inland from the Aegean sea as the location.

Schliemann visited Bunarbashi, but it did not seem right to him. The Iliad mentioned that Mount Ida was visible from the walls of Troy. From Bunarbashi the mountain could not be seen. The Iliad also mentioned that the Greek warrior Achilles chased the Trojan Hector around the walls of the city three times. Bunarbashi had a steep drop on one side that made that impossible. The distance from the sea also seemed wrong. It was eight miles where Schliemann approximated from the text that it should not be more than four.

Using geographic clues from his copy of the Iliad, Schliemann discovered another hill near the village of Hissarlik that seemed to fit the bill. The distance from the sea was right, Mount Ida was visible, and the ground around the outcropping was flat so someone could run around the walls. Schliemann did some checking and found that a couple of other people had come to the same conclusion. In 1822 Charles Maclaren of Scotland published a book claiming Hissarlik as Troy. Frank Calvert, an Englishman living in Turkey, also believed the same thing. Calvert had acquired about half of the hill.

The German was excited, but before he started digging he went to Paris for two years to study archaeology, write a book on Troy and got his Ph.D. from Rostock University in Germany. Before setting out on his dig, Schliemann decided to divorce his current wife and marry another. He wrote to a friend in Greece asking him to locate him a Greek wife. Schliemann wrote that she needed to be young, an orphan, and most importantly a fan of Homer and the Iliad. The friend found seventeen-year-old Sophia Engastromenos. When they met, Schiemann quizzed her on her Homer and she passed. The two were married in Athens. Schiemann had found his own Helen.

A firman, or agreement, was obtained from the Turkish government that would allow Schliemann to dig at Hissarlik. The agreement stated that any treasure found must be divided with the government. Excavations started in 1871 with seventy local workers. Schliemann sunk shafts and trenches into the hillside. What he discovered was not the ruin of a city, but the remains of eleven cities, each one built on the ruins of the earlier settlements.

The bottom-most city, which is referred to as Tory I, Schliemann thought must have been destroyed by an earthquake because of the cracks in the foundations. Since the Greeks had destroyed the city with fire according to Homer, this could not be the remains of the city mentioned in the Iliad. Troy II, the next layer up, had been burned. Schliemann decided that this must be the Troy of Homer's tale. The next season he hired 160 men to dig down to this layer of the hill. Scientific archaeology had not really come of age yet and unfortunately this work destroyed much of the later history of the city.

The main objective of Schliemann's work was to find what he called "Priam's treasure." According to Homer, Priam ruled the city of Troy during the war. Schliemann felt sure that the King must have hidden his treasure somewhere in the city to avoid its capture by the Greeks should they win the battle.

In May or June of 1873, Schliemann and Sophia were out at the site watching the digging when Schliemann's eye caught site of a glint of copper coming from the side of one of the shafts. Climbing down, he realized he was looking at a copper jug embedded in the wall. There was a hole in the jug and he could see gold inside. Telling his wife to send the workers on a break, Schliemann used his knife to dig in the wall and free the jug. Sophia soon joined him and they both shared in the discovery.

"While the men were resting and eating," he later wrote, "I cut out the Treasure with a large knife. This required great exertion and involved great risk, since the wall of the fortification beneath which I had to dig threatened every moment to fall on me. But the sight of so many objects, every one of which is of inestimable value to archaeology, made me reckless. I never thought of any danger."

The treasure included golden earrings, necklaces, pots of silver and gold and other items. The most impressive of these were two gold diadems that might have been worn by a queen or princess. The treasure was smuggled back to Schliemann's home and then out of the country.

The Turkish government was not amused and sued Schliemann. They won a $5,000 judgment. Schliemann at first refused to pay, but then relented and gave the Turkish government five times the actual value of the fine. The Turks decided to allow Schliemann to again dig at Troy, but this time they would watch him like a hawk.

Schliemann decided to start another dig at Mycenae in Greece which had been the home of Agamemnon, leader of the Greeks that had attacked Troy. The city had lay in ruins since 468 B.C.. Unlike Troy, the location was well-known. Schliemann cleared the gate of the city and then started digging within a strange circle of stones inside the entrance. He found 19 graves and a treasure of grave goods worth more than the cache at Troy. One of them was a golden death mask. Thinking he had found the grave of the king Schliemann said, "I have gazed on the face of Agamemnon!"

Despite all his luck at finding treasure, Schliemann was consistently wrong on his facts. Later archaeologists would date the treasure at Mycenae as being two hundred years before the time of Agamemnon and the treasure of Troy over a thousand years before Homer's Trojan War. In 1878 Schliemann returned to Troy and discovered two additional small treasure troves. In 1879 he took on an assistant, Wilhelm Dorpfeld. Dorpfeld would continue the work on Troy after Schliemann died, deciding that Troy VI was really the city of Homer's poem.

Dorpfeld would later change his mind when Carl Blegan examined the site in 1932. Blegan unearthed convincing evidence that Troy VII-a was the Homeric city. Dorpfeld, in his eighties by that time, came to agree with him.

In 1880 Schliemann, who was growing old by then, decided he needed to find a permanent home for the Treasure of Troy. He donated it to a museum in Berlin, Germany. It disappeared during WW II seized by Russian soldiers, and now resides in the Pushkin Museum in Russia.

Yes, Schliemann was very lucky. Recently some historians are asking if perhaps he was too lucky. Several incidents Schliemann wrote about in his life have turned out to be fabrications. This has made some archaeologists wonder if some of the treasure he found were actually modern forgeries planted to enhance his own reputation. Even the wonderful, but incorrectly named, "Mask of Agamemnon" has come under scrutiny. Did Schliemann fake it? Or at least alter it to appear more dramatic? For the time being the nobody has proved these things a fake and despite some falsehoods in his writings his claim that he found the city of Troy still stands.

As for Troy itself, many archaeological mysteries remain. Studies show that the people who built the first Troy were not the same people who later lived there during the Trojan War. Who were these early people and what became of them? Homer's poem suggests that the war was over the kidnaping of a Greek king's wife. It's hard to believe that the Greeks fought a ten-year war over one woman. What was the real reason for the hostilities? Legend has it that Troy fell when the Greeks built a wooden horse, filled it with soldiers and the unsuspecting Trojan's rolled it into the city. Is this true?

These questions remain as challenges to future archaeologists that would dig for treasures at the ancient city of Troy.